The Business
of Living

The Business of Living

DR. JACK H. GROSSMAN

STEIN AND DAY/*Publishers*/New York

First published in 1975
Copyright © 1975 by Jack H. Grossman
All rights reserved
Designed by Ed Kaplin
Printed in the United States of America
Stein and Day/*Publishers*/ Scarborough House,
Briarcliff Manor, N.Y. 10510

Library of Congress Cataloging in Publication Data

Grossman, Jack H   1934–
   The business of living.

   1.   Conduct of life.   I.   Title.
BF637.C5G76   158′.1   74-28223
ISBN 0-8128-1755-9

Dedication

To the very special people in my life:
My partner, friend, and wife
Joan
and our children
Lynn
Gayle
Michael
Gary

Acknowledgment

I am grateful to all the people who have helped to make my life meaningful—my family, friends, patients, and students. Special thanks are due to Sol Stein, whose encouragement made this book possible, and to Mary Solberg, whose many valuable suggestions and skillful editing added the finishing touches to it.

Contents

Part 5: IF YOU WANT A PARTNER

Part 6: LOOKING AHEAD

Part 1

YOU ARE IN BUSINESS FOR YOURSELF

1

We Are All in the Business of Living

When anyone asks me what business I'm in, my automatic response is: I'm a psychologist. But that's only a partial answer. A more accurate and complete response would be: I'm in the *business of living*.

That's the business we are all in.

Being in the business of living means, of course, that all of us, regardless of our profession or vocation, are essentially in business for ourselves. No one hires you to live, nobody can live your life for you. This business is yours alone. You are the sole proprietor.

Your job or vocation represents only a portion of this total business. It offers you the means and opportunity to earn an income. If you are fortunate, you can do it in a way that is personally satisfying. But being successful in your job, while important, doesn't guarantee success in the more complicated business of living. I have known many wealthy people—doctors, executives, politicians, and other professionals—who by most obvious standards are successful. Yet they are emotionally, socially, and intellectually bankrupt, or on the verge of it.

Jim is one of many such people I have met through my counseling practice. By age forty-nine he had built a financially successful manufacturing organization. Because his attention and energies were focused on developing this commercial enterprise, he spent as much as twelve to fourteen hours in the plant. He ignored his family and friends. And his relationships with other people were, for the most part, on a superficial level. He could not enjoy them as people; each person was either a contact or a tool, a potential extension of his firm.

His evidence of success? The obvious: money, an expensive home in the suburbs, and membership in a private club. He came to me because he felt lonely, depressed, and generally unhappy. His marriage was shattered and his children showed signs of emotional problems (one popped pills, another quit school and was unemployed, and the third was a pregnant, unmarried teen-ager).

He felt he did not have any genuine friends. Here is a man who, while successful in a commercial business, missed out on other dimensions of living that are at least as important. Because he lived for his business, that was all he wound up with. But he wanted and needed things money could not buy.

A housewife who devotes all her attention to her children and household chores, ignoring her own development, is a variation of the same problem. She may be a successful mother by certain standards, but she is also headed for bankruptcy. After the youngsters are gone, where is she?

The housewife and the company president have one thing in common: each lives a narrow and restrictive life. They may be extreme examples, but they represent real people who are denying themselves much that life has to offer.

I have met men who are not financially well off, and who do not have very responsible positions. But as far as living is concerned, they are highly productive and successful. I have also met women who are devoted to their children and their home, but who also find time to meet people, volunteer their time for worthwhile causes, travel occasionally, and attend a lecture or two.

So that we stay on the same wavelength, three important issues should be clarified. First, what do I mean by *living*, and how does it differ from surviving or existing? Second, what do I mean by *business*? And, finally, what is the *business of living*?

When these questions are answered I will elaborate on the promise this book offers, which is to help you live a rich and full life within your personal and economic limits.

Existers vs. Livers

Most people, if given a choice, would not want to die. Yet so few people choose to live. Many merely exist, survive, and mark time. Intellectually and emotionally they pass through each day, and the highlight of their day is going to sleep at night. They can't wait until the weekend, but don't know why. "Existers" tread water rather than swim. Instead of being turned on and charged up by life and its challenges, they attempt to maintain "neutrality."

Existers do what they have to primarily to avoid problems they're sure will arise if they fail to do what is necessary. Their actions are essentially defensive. They approach tasks with the attitude of "I've got to do this because if I don't, look at the mess I'll be in." They derive little joy and excitement from doing things. Their motto is, "Don't rock the boat." Even if the water becomes stagnant, at least they're safe.

Existers are escape artists. They may work extra-long hours primarily to escape from family responsibilities. They go to the movies mainly to escape from reality, and they watch television for the same reason. They go out because it's better than sitting home. You would think these would be relaxing activities. But not for existers. Their actions are motivated by choosing the lesser of two evils. They run from, rather than move toward, life and what it offers.

The exister denies reality. Like an ostrich, he hides his head in the sand; he does not admit or face up to problems. Even when confronted with facts and evidence relating to his problem, his reaction is: "I can't believe that, that's not true." If he finally comes to accept the evidence, he genuinely believes his problems will vanish—"Just give it time." Existers are not emotionally and intellectually attuned to the world around them because they live in their own narrow world. They see and hear only what they want to. The world passes them by, and they do not even realize it.

Living, on the other hand, means actively taking steps to make the most of yourself, your experiences, and your environment; it is an active process. The "liver" is not satisfied with simply going through the motions. He approaches duties, obligations, and activities with an attitude of "What benefit or pleasure can I get out of doing this?" He reaches out with a childlike excitement and hopeful enthusiasm. He looks forward to tomorrow, but does not lose sight of today and the value of the moment.

Living is taking advantage of those opportunities that can help you develop as a person. It is knowing what is good for you, and what will make you feel good, and then going after these experiences. The "liver" builds on these experiences and tries to grow and learn from them.

I am reminded of the story about a father who had two sons, one a confirmed pessimist, the other an eternal optimist. The father saw their respective attitudes expressed in many different situations, but he wasn't convinced that these attitudes were firm. So he devised what he considered the ultimate test, which he planned to conduct on Christmas.

For his pessimist son he purchased a magnificent, expensive, electric-run, made-to-order toy with all kinds of optional gadgets. He wrapped it in paper that reflected the toy's quality. For the optimist he merely got a huge corrugated box, which he filled with horse manure. He didn't even wrap it; he just taped down the top.

On Christmas morning the two boys were ready to open their gifts. The pessimist opened his box first. "Not another one of these. Look at all the gadgets. It will break before I get a chance to play with it. And the metal will rust, I know. This is just like any other Christmas. But I suppose it's better than nothing."

The optimist's turn was next. As he opened his box, his eyes lit up like a Christmas tree. Eagerly he started digging into the box. His father, perplexed by this behavior, asked, "What are you so excited about?"

Hardly pausing, the optimist replied, "With all this manure, there's got to be a pony in here somewhere."

The contrasting attitudes expressed by the two boys in the story characterize the basic difference between the exister and the liver. The liver does not deny the fact that, figuratively speaking, there is much horse manure he has to contend with. But he is excited by the prospect of finding "ponies" in his job, his other activities, as well as in his personal relationships. This prospect makes his search, as well as his find, a joyful experience. Livers have their down moments, of course. But they bounce back because they know what life has to offer. They have "been to the mountain."

The exister, on the other hand, wallows in the horse manure, continually complaining of his plight. His focus is on the manure, not on the ways to get out of it. He fails to look beyond the obvious, insensitive to the possibility that there is more to life than the ugly, narrow world he sees before him. Because he refuses to march, the big parade passes him by.

What Is a Business?

In this book the term *business* is not used in a strictly commercial sense. Rather, I use this term in two ways. First, it is *a process of handling one's affairs.* Second, it is *a concern, system, or operation which has a product or service to offer.* To be in business requires that persons (or concerns) marshal their available resources to achieve whatever objectives they have established.

While living is not structured like a commercial enterprise, there are enough similarities so that we can employ some of its vocabulary and concepts. Business terms sometimes serve as convenient ways of looking at ourselves and our experiences. Most people know, for example, that assets are plus factors, and that liabilities are a minus. Or that the major aim of businesses is to profit from being in business. We understand that in order to get dividends, you have to make investments. Business concepts can help us look at life not only for what it is, but also in terms of what we must *do* to achieve our objectives and prosper as human beings.

What Is the "Business of Living"?

The business of living is one you entered into involuntarily the moment you were born; you had no choice. You inherited some basic raw material and equipment to work with. You were also housed in an environment that influenced your thoughts and feelings about how to process your raw material.

During your early years you were taught by example, and learned from experience, what it took to deal with your particular environment. You learned by observing and listening to people close to you, as well as through your own trial and error, what was acceptable and appropriate behavior; you also learned what was considered inappropriate or unacceptable.

If you were fortunate, these influences helped you develop the foundation for a productive life. Positive input fostered in you a feeling of personal worth and value. When you matured and encountered new experiences, your good judgment prompted you to act in a way that enhanced your self-worth and contributed to your well-being.

Many people have not had this kind of positive guidance and direction in building a solid foundation for living. Their parents, often without meaning to, inflict unwholesome attitudes, anxieties, and prejudices on their children. They say and do things that confuse their offspring, or fail to encourage them. What can result is an inaccurate assessment by their youngsters of their self-worth. As they mature, these people spend a good deal of their lives attempting to overcome the scars left by their parents.

Whatever these early influences, positive or negative, you are now an adult, fully responsible for running the complicated business of your own life. What makes this business of living complicated is that its major product is *you*—a feeling, thinking, and acting human being. Vulnerable to a continually changing and demanding environment, to pressures that demand actions and decisions, you have to cope with these stresses.

Moreover, you are the result of a past that you must understand and learn to use effectively. You can't change the past; all you can do is put it in perspective so it doesn't overpower you as you live today and plan for tomorrow.

Yes, the business of living is difficult. But, you are in it. And, short of suicide, there is no way to escape it. It requires full-time attention. It can be a lonely, painfully tough, and unrewarding enterprise. Or it can be rich, meaningful, and yield high dividends.

Remember, *you are the producer as well as the product*. A product does not make itself. And producing anything requires effort. You are the one who has to decide what you want for yourself—what's going to give you what you need to feel alive and to enhance your growth and worth as a person.

Let's look at the process.

Making Your Business Thrive

Heads of thriving and profit-making businesses owe much of their success to sound and proven principles they employ in directing their operation and its people. Without these principles to guide them, decision-making and actions become haphazard, and every problem becomes a crisis. Principles serve as guideposts and reference points, governing a manager's actions and reactions and helping him define his limits so he doesn't stray too far from his objectives.

Similarly, you need to develop some basic guiding principles to manage your life effectively. It is much too precious to take for granted, drifting along with your eyes half closed. When you function primarily by "the seat of your pants," you shortchange yourself and those around you of many of the benefits your business has to offer.

You do not have to be superhuman, supertalented, super-bright, or superwealthy to live a meaningful and exciting life. Regardless of what you have, if you manage what you've got properly and judiciously, you can attain these objectives. People have made millions from small products; on the other hand, there are those who have gone bankrupt with a product whose potential was excellent. It's not what you've got that matters as much as what you do with it.

The principles I have gleaned from years of working with people as a psychologist and teacher are not necessarily new or earth-shaking. After all, people have been in the business of living for thousands of years. But I would like to share with you, in practical language, what I have learned from a variety of sources: my personal experiences and reflections, experiences and thoughts of other professionals, research findings, and just plain living.

Since all of us are basically in the same business, I believe that many of the principles that have proved valid for me and those I have counseled can also be meaningful to you. One caution: *The task of making these ideas and experiences personally meaningful is strictly up to you.* I am not about to tell you *what* to produce, or what kind of life to lead. My aim is to show you *how* you can produce what you want, assuming that what you want is to make the most of the business of living.

2

Making Your Business Count

Thousands of people get up every morning, or go to sleep at night, asking themselves: "What am I knocking myself out for? Is it all worth it? What do I have to look forward to?"

They ask these questions because somewhere along the way they have lost sight of what real living is all about. Living is not dependent solely on finding some pot of gold at the end of a rainbow. If it were, life would have little purpose for those who achieve their established objectives. It's like the person who "lives to eat." After he's filled his stomach, what is there to live for?

Nor is real living dependent solely upon other persons or things. People who say, "I live for my job," or "I live for my children," or "I live for my husband [or wife]," are at the mercy of those people and things that give meaning to their life.

Of course, these factors do give purpose to living, but they are not enough. To paraphrase a line from a popular song: You can't be right for anyone else unless you're right for you. That means your major focus should be on *you* and the attitudes you bring to your daily activities.

The business of living is a lifelong process of exploration, a journey with many possible destinations. While arriving at your destinations is important, the trip itself—the process of getting there—is what we need to focus on. Whether we're talking about a business, a journey, or living, the "process" refers to

19

moment-to-moment, day-to-day operations. Many potential rewards—emotional, intellectual, and financial—will have little meaning unless you find value in the *process*.

The extent to which you live a meaningful life depends on:

1. The degree to which you *utilize your human potential*. People need your human qualities as well as your marketable skills.
2. The degree to which you are *open to experiences*. You've got to get the most out of what you do every day.
3. The degree to which you *meet and overcome challenges*. Opportunities exist all around you, if you are willing to make the effort to reach out for them.
4. Having at least one very special person, one who really cares, with whom you can *share your thoughts and experiences*.

To find purpose in living requires that you organize your search. Let's begin by examining each of these four factors.

Utilize Your Human Potential

I recall once hearing Sam Levenson, the celebrated humorist, relate the circumstances surrounding his parents' emigration to the United States. His parents, he explained, came to this country because they thought the sidewalks were paved with gold. When they arrived they quickly realized the sidewalks were *not* paved with gold; they weren't paved at all. *They* had to do the paving.

Probably no one solicited their services. It seems more likely that they recognized the opportunities available to them, then realized that whatever abilities they had were marketable—that is, that someone who needed them would pay them to use their abilities. Armed with this knowledge and belief, they proceeded to market their services. Their belief that they were needed prompted them to search for ways to confirm that belief.

The sense of *being needed* is one of the most compelling

forces for living. Many men and women, after they retire from their jobs, become lethargic and ill because they have lost this sense. It's almost as if they were saying, "What value am I to anyone now that I can't bring home a paycheck?" These people equate their worth as persons with their job productivity.

Similarly, many homemakers whose children are grown, out of the house, and married, feel useless. Because their services as cooks, housekeepers, and chauffeurs are no longer in demand, their lives are over. Many of them make themselves emotionally and physically ill.

Age is not the culprit. Some younger people, too, get up every morning depressed. Because they have nothing to look forward to, they, too, view themselves as unimportant and unneeded objects. Their problem, like that of their elders, is that they fail to acknowledge and appreciate their total worth as human beings.

Everyone wants to feel needed, to believe, even in some small way, that others consider us important. I suspect that's one of the reasons many people own dogs, cats, or other pets. These animals need their owners for their very survival. Pet owners must feel a deep sense of obligation to know that they are in control of a life, even if it is the life of an animal.

But you can't expect people to knock on your door and say, "I need you." How can they, when they don't know who you are and what you have to offer? That feeling has to come from *you*. First you have to let others know that you have qualities and skills to offer, which they need. Then others are in a position to request your services, to *need* you.

But, you say, you have nothing of value to offer others. Or perhaps you believe that your resources are too limited to be worth anything. Frankly, neither of those beliefs is based on fact. You are not giving yourself enough credit as a human being. In the business of living, you are *the* "sales representative" of a complex enterprise. Because your business, like that of every individual, is unique, you will be surprised at how many people are in the market for your special services.

Whether you render your services to friends, relatives, people in general, organizations, or a boss, you are a salesperson of valuable commodities. Your personality, your abilities, and your humanness are desperately needed by many people.

Ask yourself, "What qualities or abilities do I have that others might be interested in? Why are my friends attracted to me? What do they see in me that interests them? If these attributes are appealing to them, are there others who might be in the market for these same qualities?"

The point is that *if someone else needs what you have, then what you have is valuable.* You become a person who is needed. Children who trade baseball cards seem to understand this concept. I've watched my own youngsters develop a sense of real power during these trading sessions when they have a card that others in the group don't. "I've got a card you don't have; what will you give me for it?" Or, "No, I don't want to trade this; it's too valuable." When others bid for their treasure, their confidence and feeling of being in demand becomes evident in their actions.

Professional and competent salespersons are masters in the art of *creating demands* for their services. One of the most successful salesmen I ever met sold insurance. In one of our many conversations, I suggested that it must be awfully difficult selling insurance policies. "Actually," he replied, "I don't sell insurance. What I sell is peace of mind, security, and all the benefits insurance offers. The policy is merely a tool through which a person can derive these benefits. Nobody is really interested in buying a policy, but people do want and need those things the policy will give them."

This attitude is shared by other good professional salespeople I have met. Each of them has told me, in one way or another, that they are selling convenience, good feelings, beauty, solutions to problems, and other benefits people need or want. Some even view themselves as good-will ambassadors. They feel needed because without them their prospective customers or clients would not know what values their products or services can provide.

If you feel you've got nothing to sell—nothing to offer—
maybe it's because you view yourself strictly in terms of your
money-producing skills. You have probably failed to realize that
even if your skills are limited, you have *human qualities* you can
offer to people who can benefit from your experiences, ideas, and
listening time. There are many people who would welcome
them, people who are less fortunate than you, people, like you
and me, who are always in the market for good and genuine
relationships.

Why haven't you thought about this approach before?
Chances are you take yourself for granted. You don't think of
yourself as having "trading cards" others may need. Once you
begin to look upon yourself as a valuable commodity, you will
find all sorts of possibilities.

A former patient of mine, a fifty-two-year-old married woman, complained of numerous aches and pains. Her physician
could find nothing physically wrong with her, she told me, but
"I'm depressed, unhappy, and there is nothing to live for any
more."

During one conversation, I discovered that she used to enjoy
sewing. She made clothes for herself and other family members.
While she was proud of her work, she felt that many people had
similar talents; she believed she was not unique.

"Look," I told her, "you have nothing to lose. Why not place
an ad in the neighborhood newspaper? Just say that you are a
dressmaker who is available at home to do alterations."

The initial calls she received were for minor kinds of sewing
work. Later, as her clientele increased, she had to limit her
activities to making new dresses. She no longer accepted what she
considered noncreative or nonchallenging work.

Her health improved within several weeks after she began. As
she put it, "I can't afford to be sick when people need me." The
recognition and appreciation she got, more than the money she
earned, made her feel needed.

Even parents whose children are out of the house and married can find value as parents. Your children may not depend on

you for the same things they needed while they were growing up. But they do need you to be proud of them; they need your emotional support; they may need you to be good and helpful grandparents; they need you to share their good fortune, as well as their problems, on an adult level. But don't expect them to tell you that they need you. You must believe it yourself, and then reach out to offer your services.

Besides those who feel they have no special talents that are needed, there are many who perceive themselves as specialists. They live in constant fear that when their particular talents go, so will they. Typically, these people do not see themselves as multipurpose, multifaceted individuals.

One man I know was firmly convinced that others were attracted to him because of his genius. When he talked to his neighbors, wife, friends, and people in general, he felt it necessary constantly to impress them with his intellect. He could not understand why people tended to dodge him.

As it turned out, he felt that his only value to people was his brain. He had not acknowledged the possibility that there was more to him than that. As a result he was essentially a lonely and unhappy person who failed to reach out.

Remember what I said earlier. You are a complex person with many dimensions and qualities. You are not *just* a breadwinner, or *just* a parent, or *just* anything. You are first and foremost a human being with many potentially "gold-paved sidewalks." But you must do the paving.

You can't afford to be dependent on any single dimension to give meaning to your life. *If you live strictly for your job, your family, or your career, you are at the mercy of the person or thing you live for.* You have to first find value and meaning in yourself. Then, and only then, will you develop the self-confidence, ability, and sensitivity to search out those vehicles that can help enrich your life.

Look within yourself for all the possible human attributes and skills you have to sell. Ask some of your friends and relatives what they see in you that perhaps you don't. Once you discover what you have to "sell," promote your services to people who you believe might be in the market. When you do, you will receive the compensation we all long for: a feeling of being needed.

Be Open to Experiences

Look at yourself. You are a thinking, feeling, and acting human being. Look at the world around you; it is an exciting adventureland waiting for you to explore it. There are so many things to see, hear, feel, and taste, so many experiences to be enjoyed.

Are you reaching out for these experiences? Or are you one of those people who gets up in the morning dreading the day, wishing it were night? Are you enjoying all the opportunities available to you? Or are you simply going through motions, performing tasks like a machine? During the course of each day do you rush from one task to another, rarely getting pleasure from your activities because you are too busy rushing?

Earlier I said that we are all salespersons offering our individual services to those who may need them. At the same time we are also purchasers of services. Think of the last time you bought something. What you bought wasn't merely a product, was it? It was something you felt would be of some potential value.

You have too much regard for your money to spend it recklessly. Nor would you, I suspect, consider giving it away unless you received something of concrete or emotional value in return. Similarly, in the business of living, you spend time during your waking hours doing things. What, of personal value, are you getting in exchange for the time you are investing? If your answer is "Very little," you are cheating yourself.

Most people go through the day performing all kinds of tasks and participating in a variety of activities. But I wonder how many look upon these tasks and activities as experiences that have personal meaning. Many people approach these tasks with attitudes like "I can't wait until it's over," or, "I really don't want to do this, but I will," or, "Isn't it terrible that I have to do this."

Their complaint, whatever it may be, suggests that they feel put upon. For all practical purposes, they view their acts as time wasted.

The differences in attitude between people who simply perform tasks and those who learn from the tasks they perform are important in the business of living. Probably the main difference is that for existers tasks are seen strictly as means toward achieving certain ends, something you have to go through in order to get what you really want. There are no benefits to be gained from the means; only the end product counts.

The living person, on the other hand, is aware that he has to perform many tasks; some he likes, some he doesn't. In either case he looks for some attractive feature in the *process* of achieving his objectives. He finds personal value in the means, while he looks ahead toward the ends. He recognizes that the time he spends in performing his tasks is valuable, so he may as well gain some benefit from it.

Recently, I had to make a one-day out-of-town business trip. The person next to me on the airplane was staring out the window. When I caught his eye, I greeted him. He didn't respond. I saw him trying to take a nap. Fine, I thought, the man is entitled to that.

When breakfast was served I again tried to initiate a conversation, but to no avail. He wasn't napping, reading, or doing much of anything but staring out the window. It appeared to me that his plane ride was strictly a way of getting from one place to another. What did he buy with his time? Nothing more than a ride.

On my return flight I sat next to another man. This person responded cordially to my greeting. We got involved in an interesting discussion about the business of living. He, being an attorney, shared some personal thoughts about this subject from the legal point of view. I learned a few things from him, and I'm sure he benefited from my ideas. We both acknowledged to each other that because of our discussion the plane ride was a worthwhile experience.

Real living is more a matter of your attitude toward your

activities than of the activities themselves. If you take the position, "Why do I have to do this?" or, "I really hate doing this, but I must because it is my obligation," you will approach tasks grudgingly and with resentment.

If you look upon what you do mainly as an obligation, it is probably because you see yourself as a giver rather than as a receiver. The persons to whom you are giving your time are burdens you must bear. It's almost as if your objective in performing an activity is to get the people to whom you feel obligated off your back.

We all know about fathers who play with their youngsters or take them to a ball game once a year because they feel they should. They go through the motions, primarily to "placate the kid." The youngster senses this attitude. As a result, neither the father nor the child enjoys himself.

On the other hand, the father who views his activities with his youngsters as valuable experiences anticipates the pleasures he will receive: a smile, good feeling for both, and some delightful verbal exchanges. He may even learn some things from his youngsters. The time he spends will yield many personal dividends.

To be open to experiences you must ask yourself, "What emotional, intellectual, or sensual values can I receive from this activity? What do I want to buy with my time?" If you think about what a task can offer you, you can find all kinds of benefits: knowledge, recognition, relaxation, affection, accomplishment, friendship—you name it. The important thing is to *look for a positive value.*

Perhaps we can learn something from advertising agencies in this regard. When advertisers promote a product, such as a soft drink, potato chips, or beer, they don't merely tell you to eat or drink their product. Like the insurance salesman we met some pages back, they promise *benefits:* if you use their product, you will have more fun, you will be a happier person. You have certain emotional-sensual *experiences* to look forward to, not merely a way to quench thirst or satisfy hunger.

How much more important this principle is in the business of living! Acting as your own "advertising agency," promote the value of the task or activity you are performing. Think about the benefits you will derive, and then sell yourself on them. Even distasteful tasks can be viewed from this perspective.

I can't tell you specifically what you should be receiving in exchange for your time. But whatever it is, the exchange should be personally meaningful. If it isn't, maybe you shouldn't be doing it.

A good friend of mine recently told me that he went to a play he had wanted to see. During the first act he realized that it was "garbage." He told his date, "If things don't change by inter-mission I'm leaving." She agreed. Sure enough, at the end of the first act they walked out. His reason? "My time is too valuable to waste it. Yes, I paid money to see the play. But why also spend time when I'm not enjoying it?"

Personally rewarding experiences give meaning to life. If you want to be a liver, you must search for these experiences. When you transform tasks and activities into experiences with meaning, they become more than mere efforts aimed at maintaining your business, keeping your ship afloat. Viewed in a negative way, on the other hand, acts are simply a series of events unrelated to you as a growing person. You pay the price in time, but are you getting your time's worth? With an "experiencing" attitude, you are doing things to maintain the present, build for the future, and savor the moment.

When you get into the habit of looking at tasks in terms of the experiences they have to offer, you will learn to reach out for *new* emotionally and intellectually stimulating activities that you probably would not otherwise have. In short, life will not be a drag. You will look toward a *variety* of sources for your expe-riences, instead of relying on some one element of your life—your job, your children, or your home.

No matter what your activity, you will no longer see yourself as a nonbenefiting observer who is just there. Look for value in your activities and you will have a compelling feeling that unless you're getting something out of them you're wasting your time.

You will also learn to get as much as you can from your time —that's living.

Meeting and Overcoming Challenges

If you were skilled at chess, bridge, tennis, or any other game, would you be enthusiastic about playing against a beginner? Probably not—it would not be a challenge.

Challenges, someone once said, *are opportunities in work clothes.* They are opportunities because they provide vehicles for demonstrating those qualities and skills you value. If you played against someone considerably less proficient than you, what would you be demonstrating? On the other hand, an opponent whose skills matched yours would be a *real* challenge.

Such an opponent would command your top efforts. To handle his strategies and counterstrategies effectively, you would develop a "game plan" to overcome obstacles that might interfere with your objective. When you embrace *any* challenge, you have to be prepared for a similar uphill, but worthwhile, struggle.

Why do livers seem to have more opportunities than existers? Responding to, instead of avoiding, challenges, they believe that challenges and problems are opportunities. They ask themselves: "How can I solve this problem?" Then they roll up their sleeves and develop a plan of action for doing it. They may not always resolve it, but they at least respond positively to it.

Whether or not you recognize and respond favorably to a challenge hinges on at least two factors:

1. The degree to which you are interested in a particular activity and its potential rewards.
2. The degree to which you feel confident that you will succeed at the activity.

You, and only you, can make these judgments.

Challenges are all around you: within yourself, in your work, in your home, in your relations with others, and in your daily activities. You can enrich your "business" by being attuned to these challenges, "invitations" to make a decision or to take some action. The decision is either to accept or to reject the proposal. If you accept you must then take appropriate steps to meet the challenge.

If these invitations are presented by others, they come disguised in a variety of forms. The most obvious are bets and dares: "I bet you can't do this or that" or "I dare you to do such and such." Some invitations come in the form of statements such as "If you had a course or two in computer programing, your chances for promotion would be much better than they are now." Sometimes challenges are implied by questions like "Do you know anyone who could help me with this difficult project?"

Self-generated challenges require that you have some idea of what you want for yourself. Do you want responsibility? Money? Friends? Recognition? What do you want to prove or demonstrate to yourself and others? What's going to give you what you want from life? To develop challenges for yourself you also need to ask yourself, "What elements in my life are causing me dissatisfaction?" Answers to your questions will point the way to challenges which, when met and overcome, will satisfy your wants and needs.

One of my friends is an attorney. While he was struggling to develop his practice, his wife asked herself, "Is there any way I could help lessen our financial burden during this building period?" Since they had two small children, she considered it impractical to get a job.

It occurred to her that there must be other young mothers in her neighborhood who felt trapped and needed time to get away. Maybe, she thought, she could start a baby-sitting service for these women. For a reasonable fee they could have their pre-school children cared for by a competent adult.

She had no difficulty getting a "full house" every weekday. By rising to the challenge this responsibility presented, she not only helped to improve their financial state but also did something that was satisfying to her.

Whether they are self-created or presented by others, challenges exact a price. The price may be time, effort, frustrations, and unforeseen obstacles. But, I ask you, can you think of any alternatives that are more gratifying?

Sharing Your Emotions and Thoughts

At our dinner table we have a nightly informal family tradition that I would like to share with you. All of the family members, usually beginning with the youngest, relate some of their significant experiences of the day. They talk about their joys, disappointments, encounters, and anything else on their minds. Those whose turn has not yet come listen attentively, because what each person says is important to him. After dinner the two oldest children frequently sit a bit longer to discuss issues and problems that may not be interesting or appropriate for the younger ones.

The quality of these informal dinner-table discussions varies from day to day and week to week because there are days when certain family members are not home for dinner. And there are evenings when some have to leave early because of personal commitments. While each family member receives individual listening time during the course of the day and week, dinnertime has become special. This is a time when everyone looks forward to listening, sharing, and just being part of an important, non-threatening, and interested group.

In a world where we are continually graded and judged, it is good to have someone with whom we can, without fear of being judged, share our inner thoughts and feelings, who accepts us for what we are. This person may be a good friend, a spouse, or a parent.

Unfortunately, many people do not have such a relationship. I have heard some seemingly successful performers, for example, state publicly that they would gladly trade part of their success for a full-time relationship of the kind I've been describing. Many search a lifetime, but are unable to find it. They may settle for superficial "marketing friendships" based primarily on a "what-can-you-do-for-me?" attitude. But these do not seem to satisfy them, or for that matter anyone else I've ever known.

For such people, the business of living is sterile and lonely. Judging from my own professional experience, this may be why many people seek therapy. My own therapeutic relationships are based on the assumption that people come to me primarily because they need to talk with and be listened to by someone who understands and accepts them as individuals. It is a nonjudgmental, noncompetitive, and nonthreatening relationship.

I recognize and respect their human, emotional, and intellectual worth. Through our special relationship they learn to understand and accept themselves, which is the first and most important step toward developing a genuine friendship with another person.

It may seem paradoxical, but in order to reach out to someone else, you must reach into yourself, recognizing your own worth. *Be kind to yourself. You deserve the very best treatment; anything less should not be acceptable to you.*

When you treat yourself with respect, you will find it impossible to tolerate disrespectful treatment from others. When you appreciate your own value as a person, you will avoid those who try to devalue you. You will find that the most meaningful sharing you do occurs with others who feel, as you do, that one must first value oneself.

From these *new* associations, based upon mutual respect, you will be able to choose one or two people with whom you can develop deeper relationships. These are the people to whom you will trust your emotions and thoughts because they will truly care about you—just as you care about yourself.

3

Being Your Own Manager

No business runs itself. *The business of living*, like a com-. mercial enterprise, *has to be managed*. Who will do it?

Do you want to let others run your life for you? Your parents did it when you were a child. But now that you're an adult, will you allow others to continue where your parents left off? Or will you take an active role and become the principal? The more willing you are to assume the responsibility for running your own business, the greater your chance of really living rather than existing.

If you fail to accept the responsibility of directing your life and managing your affairs, others will take charge. I have never seen a tail wagging a dog, but that's what I envision when I see individuals indiscriminately place themselves in the hands of other people.

Typically, these individuals take a fatalistic approach to living. They are guided by such maxims as "If it's meant to be, it will happen," or "Whatever will be will be," or "My company [boss, spouse, friend, etc.] knows what's best for me. Let them decide." It's as if they believe that everyone else is more of an expert on their life and their needs than they are. On the basis of that assumption they allow others to control them, leaving themselves in a perpetual state of confusion.

But enough of what "they" do. Let's talk about what *you* can do to manage your life effectively. *The key to being an effective manager is to be in control of yourself, your actions, and, when possible, your environment.* To be in control you must first establish standards of acceptable and unacceptable behavior directed toward you.

One vital standard is the conviction that you and the things you stand for are important. This conviction demands that you take pride in what you do, and that what you do must represent your best efforts. In short, your actions must reflect the high value you place on yourself and your judgment.

Having this standard, you must not allow others to distract you from it, for the degree to which you maintain control over yourself and your environment will depend upon how diligent you are in upholding this standard. Remember: While you cannot control how others will behave or react toward you, you *can* control yourself and your reactions toward them.

Your belief will undoubtedly be tested frequently. An example that comes to mind involves Hank, an executive with a reputable firm. Hank's boss assigned him difficult and complicated projects. That was fine; Hank could handle them. But frequently Hank needed to confer with his boss about matters that required top-management decisions. Every time Hank asked Mr. Jones for a few minutes of his time to discuss issues about the project that was bothering him, Mr. Jones would say: "I don't have time; do the best you can." So Hank would accept his boss's response and proceed as best he could.

Almost invariably, Mr. Jones found fault with Hank's solution. Hank did not recognize the trap created by his boss. By failing to provide Hank with the information he needed, Mr. Jones had weapons to find fault with Hank's work. So the boss was in control, and forced Hank to play guessing games.

My suggestion to Hank was this: "Next time Mr. Jones says that he doesn't have time for you, and to just do the best you can, uphold your position that to do your best you need certain information from him. And that you'll wait until he has time before you continue with the project. After all, how can you possibly do your best if you are in the dark?"

Hank learned that he could maintain control over his area of responsibility by not allowing his boss, or anyone else, to pressure him into turning in second-rate work. He maintained his standard that the information he needed was important; otherwise he wouldn't request it.

Another thing a good manager remembers is that *there is no shame in looking to others for help when you need it.* A well-known and highly successful company president in the Chicago area was once asked, "To what do you attribute your success?" His reply was, "I am a specialist in merchandising—that's the area I know best. Regarding the business areas I don't know about, I hire other specialists who can help me." Here's a man who accepts his own shortcomings, and recognizes that it is to his advantage to reach out for the help he needs.

How many times have you heard—or told—stories about getting lost on the way to a party? Typically the wife says: "Dear, it looks like we're lost. How about stopping at a gas station to ask for directions?" Even though he may not be in control of the situation, he responds, "I'll find my way. I don't have to ask anyone." And so they travel around, wasting much time and gas, because he feels his male pride would suffer if he asked for help. Actually he would be in greater control if he *knew* where he was going.

To maintain control over yourself you must not allow others to put you on the defensive and to create traps designed to throw you off balance. Suppose you say or do something you believe to be in your best interests. Someone says to you, "I just don't understand you or your actions." When others want you to explain your actions they are really saying, "If I were you, I wouldn't do that." Since they are not you, your actions seem unreasonable to them.

If you wish to maintain control of yourself and the situation, you may respond in one of several ways. You could say, "Why do you have to understand?" or "Would explaining my actions help you to accept them?" or "You don't have to understand, nor would I expect you to, just accept them." The fact is, others cannot be expected to view your actions, and the things that are important to you, from your point of view.

Friends, and other people who care about you, don't feel it necessary to place you under a microscope and analyze your motives; they simply accept them, recognizing that *your choices are meaningful to you.* As long as what you do is not harmful to them, it is not necessary for anyone to understand you. Chances are that if you explain your actions to anyone who is not expected to understand, even your explanations will be questioned. And you will again find yourself in a defensive position.

I don't mean to imply that you should not listen to what others have to say. An effective manager is also a good listener, receptive to other points of view. As you learn to weigh and filter the ideas and information others may offer, you will probably find some of their thoughts well worth considering. Carefully examine these ideas and facts in terms of what you believe is best for you. Then, after you have examined the pros and cons, arrive at a decision that sounds and feels right to you.

Remember, *you are the person who has to live with your decisions.* If you still have some doubt about whether you are doing the "right" thing, ask yourself, "What is the very worst thing that could happen if I were to take this action? How bad is it?" Chances are the consequences are rarely as bad as you might imagine them to be.

This principle serves as a useful guide when others make requests of you that you cannot fulfill without paying an unreasonable price. Suppose, for example, a neighbor asked you to drive him to the airport on your way to work. Let us say you honestly felt you could not, because you have some vital things to take care of at work. But, because you don't want to offend him, you tell him you will. Consider what would happen. First, you would feel resentful that he had imposed on you. Second, you would be angry at yourself for going along with his request. And third, you would be out of control because your need to please him would overpower your own good judgment.

The worst thing that could possibly happen in such a situation is that he would be angry at you. But chances are that if you simply said, "I would like to but I have some other commitments," he would accept it. You would then remain in charge of yourself and you would avoid a problem which could adversely affect future relationships.

Another way of maintaining control of yourself revolves around how you respond to what people say to you. What others say to you may be interpreted as opinions, evaluations, or judgments:

1. *Opinions* are statements of personal preferences, like "I like your sweater" or "I don't care for your wallpaper." Everyone is entitled to his or her own opinions about anything.

2. *Evaluations* are personal preferences based upon some explicit or implicit standards. These are usually given by experts or people in authority. For example, if a boss were to tell you you are doing a good job, you would assume that he has some criteria against which he is measuring your performance. The same is true of critics, professors, or anyone else whose expertise is generally valued. Your willingness to accept an evaluation depends on whether you consider the evaluator an expert in his field.

3. *Judgments* refer to rightness or wrongness. Judgmental statements usually imply a moral value one person places on another individual's behavior or attitudes. These statements generally refer to what a person "should" or "should not" do, say, think, or feel. They imply that the "judge" believes he knows what is right or wrong for another person. If you do not agree with his judgment of your feelings, you may be offended and will probably assume a defensive posture. And, of course, you will be out of control.

To maintain control over yourself you have to be your own judge. So, when others attempt to pass judgment on behavior which you believe to be in your own best interest, and is not harmful to others, take their statements as opinions rather than judgments.

Recently an acquaintance of mine told me, "As a psychologist, you should see *The Exorcist*." I do not like violent, shocking movies, and informed him that I prefer pictures that are entertaining or meaningful to me. This movie did not, in my judgment, fall into that category. He persisted, "But you owe it to yourself to see it." I responded, "That's your opinion. In my opinion the only thing I owe myself is what pleases me." The conversation ended. If I had tried to justify or explain my decisions further, I know I would have been on the defensive.

Frequently people will attempt to place you in a judgmental role by asking your advice about something. When you give them your advice, they'll argue with you. Then you feel obligated to defend your position, and before you know it you've entered into a mutually defensive argument. You can avoid that trap. Here's an example of how I did it recently.

A patient asked me, "Should I accept the raise that was given to me, or should I discuss it with my boss and tell him I'm dissatisfied?" My response was, "I can't and won't tell you what to do, but in my opinion, knowing the conditions and what you have to offer, you have little to lose by voicing your discontent." To this he replied, "But you don't understand my boss, and the kind of person he is." Recognizing the trap, I said, "I'm not telling you what to do. I'm merely offering my opinion. If you feel you must remain silent, then by all means say nothing." I wasn't about to make decisions for him and then be placed in the position of defending them. After all, how am I or anyone else to know what is right for him?

When you become aware of factors that are important to your well-being, you can change, correct, or take appropriate steps when *you* are ready, rather than when you are pressured. For if you respond only when you are pushed into action, you are likely to lose control and be forced into making poor decisions. Under these circumstances your options become limited, and you become vulnerable to the whims of others.

You need not be a "reactor," like a fireman whose sole business it is to put out fires. You may find effective means to prevent those fires. Of course, you can't anticipate all problems, but some are predictable, and those can often be handled far more easily before, rather than after, they arise.

Being in control demands that *you* pull the strings. You must not allow yourself to be a puppet. At the same time, you need not be a tyrant who demands to be treated with respect. All you have to do is to be convinced that *your responsibility, first and foremost, is to yourself and what you believe in.* Know what you stand for, and permit yourself the right to behave in a manner that will support your stance.

If you want to manage yourself and be in charge of your living enterprise, you must begin by behaving as if you know what you want for yourself. If *you* don't manage your own life, others will.

4

Doing What You Can, Knowing What You Can't

To many people the world looks like a pretty bleak place. Perturbed by what is going on around them, what they hear or read in the news, they find it difficult to understand the cruelty and thoughtlessness they see every day. Nor is it easy for them to accept the fact that many people in responsible positions lie and cheat, or that some people must scratch for a buck merely to survive. Those who share these attitudes often feel totally helpless in a world that appears at first blush to be more animal than human.

Can you save the world from these conditions? I doubt it, though I sympathize with your concern. But sympathy will not necessarily make it easy for you to live with those problems that make headlines. So let me offer you some suggestions that may help.

You Live in Two Worlds

As a person you live in two worlds. The world "out there" is one in which you are just a single individual among millions. Within this world you are, for all practical purposes, insignificant—merely one body among myriads. You can't really worry a great deal about this world, since worrying and being upset will not change anything; it will only add to your misery.

You also live in a "small world" comprising your family,

40

friends, acquaintances, and other people with whom you come in contact. That is the world over which you can have some influence. The manner in which you conduct yourself, the way you treat your fellow humans, and the judgment you employ in managing your life can serve as a model for others to follow. By treating your friends, neighbors, and other people in your life the way you would like to be treated—with consideration and dignity—you can indirectly influence their reactions to you. You can also teach, guide, and influence your children to become the kinds of persons you would like them to be.

If you concentrate your efforts on your small world, you may in time make a contribution toward the larger one. But remember, your major thrust must be with your own immediate world. By focusing your energies on an area which is within your sphere of understanding and influence, your sense of helplessness will diminish. Your efforts will give you a feeling of importance, something the large world can't offer you.

Of course, you do have two other alternatives. You could, as so many people do, retreat into your shell and develop a "what's the use?" attitude—just continue griping about the state of the world and the people in it. That attitude will only drain you emotionally until you become bankrupt. Or you could adopt an attitude of "If I can't fight them, I'll join them" and be one of the crowd you previously criticized. In good conscience, could you accept that course of action?

The only strategy for living that makes sense to me is this: *Seriously concern yourself about things you can control or influence.* Spending time and energy wishing and hoping for human and social changes that are not within your power or capacity to change is not reasonable. Allowing these uncontrollable factors to frustrate and paralyze you emotionally can only interfere with your business of living.

At the same time, the problems you hear and read about, even though you can't change them, can stimulate you to alter and guide your own behavior. These large-world happenings can serve as excellent tools for learning and for tempering your own actions as well as those of individuals who are part of your small world.

Let's say that you're driving along on an expressway, and a reckless, speeding driver gets stopped for going too fast. You obviously can't do anything about that driver's irresponsible behavior. But his actions, and the fact that he was stopped, might stimulate you to look at your gauge, and to slow down if you are also driving a bit too fast. Similarly, while you can't do anything about the world's energy crisis, you can teach your family members to conserve energy in your home.

You can satisfy your social conscience, and possibly make contributions to the large world, by beginning with yourself and your immediate environment. You can expand your small world by joining and becoming active in local groups and associations that stand for the values and ideals you consider important. These local organizations can provide you with an arena where you can be heard and make your influence felt. Opportunities are always available to volunteer your time and efforts in causes that interest you. Remember, you are not the only one who is concerned with the state of the world. But you've got to search for suitable avenues to make your contributions.

This principle or strategy for living makes sense even in building a commercial enterprise. The owner of a quality department store may be in competition with a discount store housed on the same block. Should the quality-store owner lower his standards or give up his business? Since he can't change his competitor's practices, his only productive course of action is to develop a marketing strategy consistent with his values and philosophy. If he wants to increase the flow of traffic in his establishment, he needs to clarify the distinction between the two stores. He can do this by offering better service and more dependable products, as well as by promoting the merchandising values he stands for.

With some variations the same approach is available to anyone who is a member of a professional group. For example, the field of psychology, like medicine, law, or accounting, consists of incompetent as well as competent practitioners. Recognizing that I have no influence or control over psychologists who do not do justice to a field I am proud to be part of, what are my options? Do I leave my profession, or do I do my best and try to elevate the image of my field? Since the world of psychology is much too large to tackle, the only alternative is to focus on my immediate world.

To put the principle in business language, you've got to *pick your market*—the people you can indirectly or directly influence—rather than worrying about a market that is not within your reach.

You may not like what you see and hear in the larger world. But giving up on your own business and adding to the social pollution aren't emotionally healthy ways of coping with these problems. The only way I know of dealing with these difficulties is to ask yourself, *"What can I do in my small world to help overcome the problems of the big world?"* Then do what you can within your own limits. Focus on the possibilities available to you, rather than on your helplessness.

Coping with Your Limitations

Limits are a fact of life. You have them, I have them—we all do. Factors in the world around us restrict all of us. Similarly, each of us has personal limitations which we must live with: intellectual abilities, personal economic conditions, physical appearance, and health, to name a few. Although limitations restrict our actions and opportunities, within them we also have considerable freedom. Without any limits there is no freedom, only anarchy.

Those who continually fight and complain about their limits, while ignoring the possibilities available to them, have real problems. I can almost hear them saying, "If I only had this or that, or, when such and such happens, things would be different."

I'm not suggesting that you shouldn't try to expand your limits. We all want more freedom and opportunities, and we must work toward achieving them. But to fight our limits, while passing up those things we can accomplish within our sphere of capabilities and with the freedom we do have, makes little sense.

We have all encountered people like the salesman who says, "If I can't have a larger territory, I won't sell." He could, of course, continue to function within the territory available to him while pushing to expand it.

An elementary-school art teacher I know once described to me the different types of attitudes exhibited by various pupils in her class. Among those who could not afford the large box of paints, there were two kinds of pupils. One type refused to paint if he or she did not have a particular color. These youngsters invariably complained about what they lacked. They did hardly anything, even with the paints they had.

The other group somehow found ways to utilize the few colors they had. They learned, for example, to blend blue and yellow to make green. These students used imagination in working within their limits and found that the limits expanded as they worked with them.

This teacher also described another type of student who, despite having a complete set of paints with all the equipment money could buy, still found something to gripe about. They always wanted more, but failed to utilize what they had.

These youngsters have their counterparts among adults. Complaining about what they don't have and what others do have seems a full-time preoccupation. It certainly is a way of avoiding responsible and productive action.

You Can't Change the Past

Many people insist on making their parents, their upbringing, and their misfortunes of yesteryear their scapegoats for messing up today and tomorrow. As I've said before, we all have our scars. But does the process of tearing open old wounds for its own sake serve any worthwhile purpose? Does beating our breasts about yesterday's problems help make *today* purposeful and pleasant?

Or does such action merely give people excuses for dodging their present responsibilities?

Can you imagine a proprietor of a store saying, "Since business was bad yesterday, it will probably be bad today. Why bother coming to work?" Of course not. If he were guided by that reasoning, he would be perpetuating a bad situation. By not coming to work today, what chance does he have of overcoming yesterday's problems?

Let me illustrate my point by asking you to participate in an experiment. Walk from one end of your house or apartment to another while looking back. Keep your head turned and don't look forward. What happened? Chances are you bumped into things and tripped all over yourself. I suspect you didn't make much headway because you couldn't see what was in front of you.

What value, you ask, does the past have for today's business of living? It is a benchmark that provides some perspective for moving forward. Reviewing the past can provide us with some clues about why certain things, both good and bad, happened in our life, about what you should avoid, as well as what actions should be repeated. *Reflecting on the past is healthy only if it helps you chart your future.*

But if you want to move forward, you can't focus on or live in the past. To continually look back at where you've been, without looking ahead to where you want to go, is self-defeating. The unwholesome ghosts of your past, be they parents, teachers, bosses, friends, or painful experiences, will haunt and destroy you if you let them.

Our personal histories, particularly if they are loaded with negative experiences, can be the basis of fear and distrust. The reasoning goes something like this: "I failed yesterday, therefore I will fail tomorrow." One reason athletes go into slumps is that their confidence is shaken by fear that they will repeat past mistakes. Still another type of reasoning, possibly subconscious, is this: "My father [or mother] mistreated me, therefore all people in authority are to be mistrusted and feared." Both of these kinds of thinking block productive action.

You are in the business of living today, and building for tomorrow. Do you want to let all your yesterdays infest the future, which, at this moment, is untarnished? You don't have to, you know. Tell yourself, "Today is a new day, make it count. I can't change yesterday, and getting upset about it will not erase it." Then ask yourself, "What actions can I take today that will move me forward in the direction I want to go?"

In the final analysis *the choice is yours:* move forward and develop a strategy for living today in a world you can control and influence, or bemoan your past misfortunes, the state of the world, and your limitations, none of which you can directly control.

If you choose the latter approach, you will be in a continual state of bitterness and on the verge of bankruptcy. The more logical choice, if you are to make your business profitable, is to adopt the attitude that the only world that really counts is the one within your scope of influence and control.

Part 2

DEVELOPING A PROFITABLE BUSINESS

5

Know Yourself—
You Are Your
Most Important "Product"

An individual who believes he has a worthwhile product or service to offer, and who feels there is a potential market for his offerings, might form a business. His decision requires careful thought, preparation, and capital. He would certainly not consider embarking on this venture without knowing all about his wares and services. Yet this is exactly the situation in which you and I have been placed.

The decision to enter the business of living was not ours to make. We were thrust into it; in some cases it was purely accidental. How can we discover what we have going for ourselves, so that we receive the maximum benefits from this enterprise?

The process of getting to know yourself is never-ending. Do you recall the first time you heard yourself on tape? You couldn't believe the voice was yours. Or what about the times you rose to challenges you didn't think you could handle? Have you learned a new skill you never thought you would develop? These discoveries you made about yourself should have added to your knowledge about the kind of person you are. The fact is that your experiences, education, and relations with others help you to discover qualities and abilities that are part of you.

But if these abilities are to have any marketable or personal value, you first need to identify them as important tools and attributes for the business of living. You must consciously incorporate them as part of your "skills for living" inventory, which you can draw upon when the need arises. Unfortunately, many people don't do this. Because they take themselves and their experiences for granted, these individuals fail to acknowledge the skills they utilize every day, as well as their new discoveries.

When I have asked such people, "What do others like about you?" they respond, "I don't know what there is to like." Sometimes I say, "I very much want to like you. Could you help me out by telling me what there is about you that is likable?" Again, they respond, "I'm just like anybody else—nothing special."

Let me ask *you* a question. Suppose you were being interviewed to determine your capabilities for running a business— say, your own business of living—and the interviewer asked you, "What do you have to offer?" What would you say?

To begin with, let me reiterate what this business is all about. It is making the most of yourself and getting the highest emotional, intellectual, and financial returns possible from whatever investments you are capable of making. Getting to know what you have available to invest is your primary task for effective management. Since what you have to invest is you, that's who you have to get to know.

If you are conscientious about obtaining this knowledge, I can help you. We will divide this self-assessment project into two parts. In the first part you will examine your *functional value;* the second part will deal with your *personal-emotional side.*

Your Functional Value

From the functional point of view, you are what you do. For that reason it is important to know what services you can render that will enable you to earn your keep. As I mentioned earlier, we are, functionally speaking, no different from children who exchange trading cards. Those most adept at this trading game look at themselves in terms of what cards they can cash in for the things they want in life.

When you are ready to begin this audit, take out several sheets of blank paper on which you will write down your answers to those questions I will ask. (It would be helpful if you took time out to do this now.) If you like, you can label this portion of your audit "Functional Resources."

First, think about all the courses you had in school. In which subjects did you do particularly well? What subjects came easiest to you? Now, answer this question: What kinds of subjects did you especially like reading about? As long as you're thinking about school, consider your extracurricular experiences. If you participated in such activities, can you point to things you did which might be viewed as accomplishments?

I cannot emphasize too strongly the need to be candid in responding to these questions. Don't be modest; no one but you will look at your lists.

Next, think about the jobs you've had, the things you do and have done around the house, and any other "doing" experiences that come to mind. Out of all these experiences, what kinds of things have you done well? It is vital that you make this list exhaustive—include everything. Anything you have done well, be it in your job, in the community, or on the domestic front, counts as a functional resource.

At this point you might ask yourself, "How do I know if I've done a good job?" To this I would say, if others have complimented you on a particular achievement, chances are you've done it well and you're entitled to be proud of it.

What skills have you effectively developed over the years? You might want to consider such skill areas as: social, verbal, manual, domestic, organizational, and problem-solving. Under each of the broad categories, or any others that come to mind, describe in specific terms the skills you have successfully employed.

For example, under the "verbal" category you could include such things as: "I am convincing, and can bring people around to my point of view." Under the problem-solving category you might say, "I am able to examine the relevant facts and issues of a problem, and arrive at practical alternatives." As evidence of your social skills you could perhaps say, "I am tactful and diplomatic in relating to people; they are willing to share their problems with me."

Enough examples. I trust you have a general idea of how to go about answering this question. You will be surprised, when you finish, at how skilled you really are. All it takes is some serious thinking about yourself to realize that you have a great deal to offer your business.

Notice that I have deliberately avoided asking you to list those abilities which you do not have. My reasoning is that since you probably spend much time thinking about these anyway, it makes no sense to focus on them now.

Your final step in assessing your functional value is to examine all the abilities you have identified and then answer these questions: "To what use can you put these skills? What persons or organizations might be in the market for the skills you have available?" List *all* the outlets you can think of. It may be that you will need several outlets to demonstrate your skills. That's okay, too, since these diverse experiences will add to your wealth in the business of living.

Your Personal-Emotional Resources

If the value of an object were solely dependent upon its usefulness, the pet industry, for one, would be in sad shape. Don't you know individuals who own pets simply because they're "nice to have around"? *You* can also be enjoyable company even if your functional value to others is minimal.

There are many people I know who can't *do* anything for me, but they are individuals whose company I enjoy. These are people who give me pleasure by simply *being* themselves. They may be attractive, interesting conversationalists, amusing, pleasant, or exciting. They possess personal and emotional qualities which are human and, therefore, worth experiencing.

While the personal-emotional side of the human product is

too complex to get to know fully, it is essential that you at least begin. Why? Many people become involved in situations which they are unable to handle emotionally—because they don't know themselves: their emotional tolerance, needs, interests, and other important aspects of their being. They miss out on exciting opportunities for the same reason.

It is interesting that when people buy a pet, a plant, or any other living thing they will inquire about the nature, as well as the care and feeding requirements, of what they purchase. Yet many humans will go through life knowing less about themselves than about a plant or a pet. So that you can fill this void, my aim in this section is twofold: (1) to help you sort out your personal-emotional strengths and weaknesses; and (2) to help you become more selective or discriminating in your decisions about which activities and people to become involved with.

You will need several sheets of blank paper for this project. At the top write the phrase "I am." Now, complete it with as many adjectives or descriptive phrases as you can think of which characterize you as a person. Try to focus on your positive qualities, but don't ignore your weaknesses. Also, when thinking about who you are, consider the kinds of terms your friends and relatives have used in describing you. For example, you might write, "I am understanding, I am attractive, I am dependable, I am impatient, etc."

After you have completed your list, which may take several hours or even days to do, put a plus sign next to the positive attributes and a minus sign next to the negative ones. Now, look over the list and focus your attention on the favorable qualities. These are the ones which distinguish you as a worthwhile human being. They are your "personal strengths," which nobody can take away from you. Since these are the qualities in you toward which others are attracted, exhibit them in a variety of situations. Don't deprive people of the opportunity to enjoy this side of you.

Your "personal weaknesses" are also important, but for different reasons. By admitting to them you have taken a major step forward. The next step is to ask yourself, "Is there anything I can do to overcome these shortcomings, and, if so, what?" This question will at least get you thinking about dealing with these weaknesses. In time, you will hopefully be able to develop a "new and improved" product.

Let's now talk about your interests. Many people deprive themselves of activities they truly enjoy, while they invest an inordinate amount of time doing things they don't particularly like. These are people who respond more to social pressures than to their own desires.

Harriet is such a person. If a neighbor asks her to go shopping, she will, even though she doesn't like to. She also accepts invitations to participate in school and church functions which are not appealing to her. She just can't say no. But she complains a lot about not having time for herself and the things she likes to do.

How about *you?* How much time do you spend in activities that are distasteful to you, as opposed to those that are interesting or fun? To get at the answers to this question I would like you to write at the top of another sheet of paper the words "I enjoy." Then complete this phrase with descriptions of things you like to do. You may include such things as reading, watching television, gardening, traveling—you name it.

Look over this list carefully and ask yourself, "Of all the activities I've mentioned, which of these do I participate in as often as I would like? What specifically can I do to involve myself more in activities that give me pleasure?" Life is much too short to deprive yourself of doing those things.

I have known many people, as I suspect you have, who talk about what they would like to do "someday." But "someday" never comes or, when it does, they are old and tired. Chances are that if you think about how you can fulfill your desires, and if you become more selective in the kinds of activities you agree to participate in, you will have plenty of time and energy to do the things you like.

Some of the demands placed on your free time may not be to your liking. But they are obligations you feel you must honor.

Put these obligations in perspective and keep them to a minimum. Remember, you don't have to respond favorably to every request people make of you—even if the people are family members. What you must constantly keep in mind is that *your* pleasures are at least as important as those of others.

Another important factor you need to consider is the kinds of relationships you want to encourage, and those you want to discourage. By the way, this is an issue that companies have to contend with all the time. They ask themselves, "What kinds of customers [or clients] should we do business with, and which type of customer should we not become involved with?"

Since you can't be all things to every person, and because some people are emotionally and intellectually better for you than others, you also must exercise some discrimination in your choice of relationships. On the top of a fresh sheet of paper write, "I need to be around people who." On another sheet write, "I cannot tolerate people who." Now, describe those two types of people.

Now, think about the people you currently associate with. Are you holding on to relationships you ought to discourage because these people are making your life miserable? What can you do to develop relationships that are stimulating to you? You may, as some people I know have done, join groups or organizations where you might more readily meet the kinds of people you want to associate with. These are people who probably have interests similar to yours.

The point is that if you encourage relationships with people whom you enjoy, and discourage those you don't like, you increase the likelihood of functioning more effectively. You *can* be the person you really are, rather than the one you might be forcing yourself to become. If, at this point, you are asking yourself, "Why should these people associate with me?" go back to the lists you made describing your positive qualities. Those are the attributes you can share with others.

If you have been diligent in making these lists, you now know yourself better than you did before you started. These projects enabled you to compare what you've got going for you with what you're actually using. As a result, you are probably more sensitive to your strengths—the functional and human value of your product.

Hopefully, you discovered a person who can succeed in the business of living. If not, at least you know some of the things you can do to make your business into a successful venture.

6

What Do You Want from Your Business?

No profit-making concern can afford to drift aimlessly wherever the currents take it. While many companies look as far as five years down the road, they modify their objectives every year because the nature of their business changes, as do market conditions. But they always have some long-range goals to shoot for. Many firms also set daily, weekly, and monthly objectives. Manufacturers have production goals, department stores have sales quotas, and service organizations set up special, sometimes less concrete, goals.

In the business of living meaningful objectives can also maintain our interest and stimulate us to move forward. Many people are on the verge of bankruptcy because they fail to set concrete—and attainable—goals. These individuals spend their lives chasing rainbows and hoping for some miracle that will save them from their humdrum existence. But they don't know specifically what they are searching for.

When I ask people, "What do you want out of life?" most say things like "I want to be happy," or "I want to be successful," or "I want peace of mind." Pursuing my question further, I then ask, "What has to happen, or what do you need to achieve, for you to realize this blissful state?" In response to this question, the "rainbow chasers," wanderers, and existers describe goals that are either unrealistic or so distant that they may never be realized.

Bertha's response typifies the kind of reaction I'm talking about. "What would make me happy," she said, "is not to have any worries or concerns and to be able to do anything I want with my time."

"Suppose," I replied, "I could wave a magic wand and free you from all worries and time commitments. What would you do with your life so that you would be happy?"

"I don't know," she said. "But it would be something nice to think about."

People like Bertha, whose desires are expressed in such vague and unrealistic terms, are deluding themselves. Life does not give anyone happiness, success, or peace of mind. *All life can offer you is the opportunity to live—*to be in business. Perhaps a more appropriate question is, "What do you want from yourself so that you can be happy, feel successful, and achieve peace of mind?" This question places the burden on ourselves rather than on some abstraction we call life.

No company president would deny that he is in business to make a profit, and I am certainly not denying that happiness, success, and peace of mind are worthwhile goals. But unless you determine which specific roads you want to travel—unless you establish objectives, both short- and long-range—you will continue to wander through life without realizing many emotional, intellectual, and financial returns. It's all part of the master plan to achieve the profits you want from your business.

You will gain at least three benefits by defining your goals. First, clearly stated objectives *indicate what specific courses of action you need to take* to accomplish your goals. For example, one of my objectives in writing this book was to complete it within a certain time period. With this in mind, I knew what I had to do every day to progress toward this goal.

Objectives also *provide incentives to achieve your goals.* When you know *why* you are doing something, you are more willing to pursue an activity. A friend of mine goes twice a week to the local Y.M.C.A., and swims one mile each time. When I asked him why he pursued this activity, he said, "I want to be a member of the fifty-mile club. This is a club consisting of individuals who swim a total of fifty miles within a six-month period." If my friend didn't have this or some similar goal to shoot for, he might not be as determined to go as regularly as he does.

Finally, establishing objectives *enables you to judge the propriety of your actions.* Objectives provide you with some basis for eliminating activities that do not contribute to accomplishing your goals. You can guard against the feeling that was so well expressed by one of my patients, who said, "I can be so busy, yet feel terribly empty inside." Frequently this empty feeling develops when objectives are hazy and actions have no direction. On the other hand, you will feel good about yourself when your activities contribute, either directly or indirectly, toward achieving your objectives.

We are now ready to pursue, in more specific terms, the question, "What do you want from your business?"

Establishing Long-range Objectives

Each proprietor has to establish reasonable goals that relate to his own enterprise. Goals imposed by relatives, well-meaning friends, or other people who seem to know what's "best" for you have no place here. Remember, this is *your* business we're talking about, nobody else's.

To help you get started, let's use as a guideline three of the four factors, discussed in Chapter 2, which give purpose to life. You may recall that the first requirement for living a full and meaningful life is to *utilize your potential.* Keeping this general factor in mind, what specific goals can you establish which will help you do this? Think in terms of a specific time frame—say a six- or twelve-month period. Then write your objectives down.

This is not as difficult as you may think. From what you did in the previous chapter, you already know much about the nature of your "product." Now what you have to do is decide what goals you want to accomplish with what's available to you.

You might, for example, set some educational objectives. If

you do, be specific about what courses you want to take, or what kinds or how many books you would like to read. There are many ways in which you can utilize your potential besides formal self-improvement courses. It might be helpful if you asked yourself the question I raised earlier: "What do I want from myself during the next year?" Or "What do I want to accomplish in this period that will give me personal satisfaction?"

After you have written your goals under this particular category, consider the second criterion for living a meaningful life: *What goals can you set that will add significantly to your experiences?* Again, be specific about what you want to accomplish.

You will be pleasantly surprised by all the things there are to do and see once you spell out your objectives. One man I know wrote down as one of his goals: "During the next twelve months I will make it a point to visit every museum and attend every exhibit that is available." He did this on weekends, and when the time he allowed himself was up, he still had not seen everything there was to see. He could not believe there were so many opportunities in his own city that were not only enjoyable but also inexpensive.

While I can't tell you what kinds of experiences to aim for, the possibilities are numerous. This is a good time to ask yourself, "What kinds of experiences are available to me that might benefit my business?" Write these down as goals to accomplish.

Finally, you can look for objectives to shoot for in the "challenges" category. For example, I know of men who consider it a goal to maintain their health. These are people whose jobs require little physical energy. In meeting this challenge they establish as one of their objectives "to go to a gym two or three times a week."

Women may have similar challenges, or they may be like Gail, a mother of five children, all under twelve years of age, who told me that maintaining her sanity was a goal. And so she engages in a variety of adult activities which enable her to achieve her long-range objective. She belongs to a women's club and a reading circle that meets once a month. She is also active in a gardening club. She finds stimulating things to do so that she can be a happier person, and therefore a better mother, rather than a resentful one.

Establishing Short-range Objectives

The business of living is a *daily* process. Unless you have things to look forward to doing today, things that are satisfying in themselves, but also bring you nearer to what you want tomorrow, you are wasting the day. Can you afford to do that?

"What do I want from myself *today* that will move me closer toward each of my objectives?" That is the question we have to contend with on a day-to-day basis.

Let's take the person who says, "I want to be successful." Of this individual I would ask, "What can you do *today* which will make you feel successful for at least this twenty-four-hour period?" Why, you might ask, is today so important? Because it is all any of us really have. Yesterday is gone, and tomorrow we are not sure about. All we can really count on is the present. If you miss out on that, it becomes just another yesterday.

I don't know of any commercial enterprise that could tolerate too many nonproductive days. Once they open their doors for business, overhead costs begin to add up and they must somehow cover these expenditures. We, as human enterprises, also expend energy of all sorts during a day. Why not get something in return for our investments?

Daily objectives help to structure our time. If we know what we want to achieve this day and this week, we can go about the business of accomplishing these short-range goals. Perhaps another question that might help you focus on the value of the day is to ask yourself, "Why do I want to live today?"

Because it is easy to let your days and weeks pass with nothing of real value to show yourself for having lived that period, it is important to list those things you want from yourself every day. Use your list of long-range goals as a guide. If, for example, one of your long-term objectives is to lead a more relaxed and less hectic life, you should allow some time *today* for relaxation. Or, if you want to develop a particular skill, you ought to allow some time *today* for practicing that skill.

A problem many people run into is that they lack patience in following through on long-range objectives. Their lament is, "It'll never happen, so why bother?" They start a project enthusiastically, and work diligently for several days toward achieving their goals. But their enthusiasm is short-lived and they quit. To these people I have a personal story to relate that illustrates an important principle regarding goal attainment.

Several years ago I decided to grow tomatoes in our back yard. I heard that it was easy to do, and the thought of being able to have fresh, homegrown tomatoes appealed to me. I bought six plants and planted them according to the salesman's general instructions. Several weeks went by, but no tomatoes. I waited a bit longer, but still no fruits—just large plants.

My patience diminished substantially, and I began to lose interest in the project. By the end of the summer all I had to show for my meager investment was an ugly weed patch and a few small, bug-infested green tomatoes. The project was a flop.

Later that year I discussed my experience with a friend of mine who boasted that he had a large yield. "It was one of the best crops I ever had," he said. When I related my problem, he told me that growing tomatoes requires patience and regular, diligent effort. He gave me specific instructions on what to do next time I decided to grow them.

The following spring I vowed that I would have a respectable tomato yield, and that nothing was going to stand in my way. I started out about the same way as I had the previous year. But this time I fertilized the plants, watered them regularly, and sprayed them for bugs. After a number of weeks the plants bloomed, and later some green tomatoes sprouted.

While there was nothing edible yet, I was convinced that if I kept at it, eventually my objective would be achieved. It finally happened. One morning I spotted two beautiful red tomatoes. My perseverance and determination were beginning to pay off.

By the end of the summer we had an unusually large yield. I have followed the same procedure since that eventful year, and have not been disappointed.

The important lesson I learned from my two contrasting experiences was this: when you set a goal, you have to work at it regularly to achieve it. If you maintain your pace, and do all that is necessary along the way toward your goal, eventually the goal will become an accomplishment.

It is natural to become discouraged when the fruits of your labor do not materialize quickly. But you have to believe that if you keep your eye on your long-range goals, and work toward them every day or week, you will get what you want from your business—today as well as tomorrow.

7

Planning for Living

Living is the business of making desires and dreams come true. It is the business of converting to reality your feelings and thoughts about how you want to spend your life. Simply making resolutions and promises to yourself—"I will try harder," or "I will do better next time," or "Someday I will be successful"—is not enough. Living is too complicated and changeable to merely hope for dreams and goals to materialize. If you want a profitable venture, you must plan for it; you must also develop strategies for executing your plans.

Planning increases the likelihood of accomplishing your objectives, however minor they might seem. It can be used in all kinds of activities. I recall hearing a former employer of mine, who happened to be active in politics, announce one afternoon that he was heading a committee in an upcoming political convention. "I'm in charge of planned 'spontaneous' demonstrations," he said.

"*Planned spontaneous* demonstrations?" I asked. "Isn't that a contradiction?"

"You can't leave important matters like demonstrations to chance," he explained. "They can be chaotic if they are not properly organized. But, we also want them to appear spontaneous. Someone has to plan and coordinate these demonstrations to make sure they come off well. We must determine what cues we will respond to, what we will do, and how much time we will take. They have to look natural and smooth if they are to be effective."

His explanation reminded me of many people I have known who failed to get what they wanted from themselves and their environment because they didn't plan. They may know what they want to accomplish, but they don't think about how to go about realizing their objectives. As a result, their actions are haphazard and lead to confusion rather than results.

You've already taken two important steps in the planning process. Specifically, you have some idea of who you are, that is, the kind of "product" you have available. And you also have some idea of the goals you are striving for. Having established, at least in a general way, *who* you are and *what* you want, the question we have to deal with is, *How can you achieve the objectives you desire?* While I touched on this subject in the previous chapter, the question of how to plan for results, as well as how to implement your plans, merits special consideration.

To begin with, let me briefly define what I mean by planning and explain the necessity for it. *Planning is a design for getting a person from a particular starting point to some established and clearly defined goal.* It involves all the thinking that takes place prior to action. Carefully drawn plans help business leaders to think ahead, anticipate changes, and consider alternatives in case their original plans fall through.

Because businesses need to be dynamic to grow, one thing they must count on is change. Constantly changing economic conditions, technology, and customer needs and wants, whether they change suddenly or gradually, are anticipated, and plans are developed to deal with them. Recognizing that changes are inevitable, executives of forward-looking enterprises diversify and look for new opportunities. Many have research-and-development departments that work at formulating new and relevant products or services. That's the only way they can stay on top of competition and maintain their stability.

The business of living is also dynamic. Your interests, personal needs, tastes, and financial status have undoubtedly fluctuated over the years. Have your plans kept up with these changes, or are you functioning on the same level as you always have? When you fail to plan for the future you are allowing circumstances to dictate your actions. Because you are caught off guard, your reactions may be impulsive and self-defeating.

I have seen women who become emotionally and intellectually disarmed because they fail to plan what they will do with their lives after their children grow up. And what about all the men who, as a result of automation, have been displaced and find themselves vocationally helpless because they failed to plan for this possibility? Both these groups of people represent individuals who assume that the world stands still—that nothing will alter their comfortable and secure state.

Planning, particularly if you put your thoughts down on paper, also *helps to prevent oversights and mistakes.* It relieves the pressure of continually thinking about what has to be done next in the process of achieving your goals. Advanced thinking as to how you will go about doing those things reserves your energies for purposeful action rather than spinning your wheels.

Finally, *planning can be effectively employed in changing habit patterns you dislike.* Habits are customary ways of acting; they are things we normally do without thinking about them. If you want to displace a habit you dislike with one that is more appealing to you, a plan of action can help you. We will look at an example of how this can be accomplished later in this chapter.

There are essentially four elements to the "planning for living" process. First, you need to *evaluate your present conditions in relation to your future goals.* You've already done some of that if you followed the audit suggestions contained in the previous two chapters. But, you might also consider and write down your responses to the following questions:

1. What are you currently dissatisfied with?
2. As of this moment, what do you want to change?
3. Based upon your current thinking, what do you anticipate

will happen that might cause you dissatisfaction in the next two, five, or ten years?

These questions, as well as those you responded to earlier, will help you focus on your current and anticipated needs.

Second, for each of the changes you want to effect, or goals you want to achieve, you need to *develop a set of procedures.* These are the steps you have to follow in realizing the results you want. They are, in effect, a set of explicit instructions to yourself as to how you will go about accomplishing your objectives systematically. Write down all the things you have to do so that you can get to where you want to go. This step-by-step procedure will help you move forward in an orderly fashion.

As part of this procedure it is important that you evaluate each step. You have to ask yourself, "Can I do it? Do I have the information, tools, finances, time, or whatever is necessary to take this step? If I don't, what has to happen before I *am* able?" These questions will help you focus on *"How* can I do it?" rather than making excuses for "Why I *can't* do it." You will undoubtedly encounter roadblocks along the way toward your destination. But working out ways of getting around or through them is part of planning.

Third, *consider the time available to you.* How long do you estimate it will take to achieve the goal you are shooting for? You might also assign specific time periods to each step of your plan. Setting deadlines for yourself increases your sense of urgency in getting something done. It also forces you to pace yourself and to organize your time realistically. *Deadlines are excellent motivating forces.* By the way, it is better to overestimate than to underestimate the time it will take you to accomplish an objective. That way, you leave yourself a safety margin in case you need one.

Finally, your plans should *include a set of policies, general guidelines that define the boundaries within which you are determined to function.* They help you make decisions, yet stay within the limits you establish. In short, policies are your "official" attitudes which spell out the range of behavior within which you will permit yourself and others to act. Because they are broad, they leave room for judgment.

Well-defined and practiced policies leave no doubt as to where you stand and what you stand for. Companies typically have policies that guide all their operational and administrative functions. For example, an organization that has an employment policy of "promoting from within" knows exactly what to do when a vacancy occurs in the company. They first search exhaustively for individuals within the company to fill the position. A marketing policy might be: We will design products which appeal only to low-income families. If someone in the organization came up with an idea for a product too expensive for the targeted market, this policy would strongly suggest that he modify it for the appropriate market.

In formulating your plans to accomplish a goal, the policies you establish might be in the form of do's and don'ts. For example, suppose you had a goal to complete a particular project by the end of the month. One of your policies would be not to accept any time-consuming commitments during that period. Another could be that you would devote so many hours a day to it. These policies would serve as guidelines for making decisions regarding any requests or nonproject-related demands that might arise.

To demonstrate how planning actually works, I'd like to share with you how a friend of mine went about losing twenty-five pounds. Ted, like so many people, was frustrated that he could not lose weight. He tried fad diets of all sorts, none of which worked for him. What really upset him was that he didn't think he ate that much. But the fact was in front of him—an ugly bulge.

One day, stimulated by something he read in the newspaper, he decided to go about his weight-losing project in a systematic manner. He purchased a little notebook and a calorie counter. On the first day of his program he listed in his notebook everything he ate—regular meals, snacks, and anything he put in his mouth. That night he looked up in his calorie counter all the foods and beverages he had listed. Next to each item he entered the number of calories contained in it.

To his amazement he had actually consumed five thousand calories during that day. It surprised him because he was not aware of having overeaten. Apparently he had developed a habit of not thinking about what he ingested until after he had indulged himself. He felt he had to replace his gluttonous habit with a more reasonable eating schedule.

After overcoming his shock, he set down a plan to follow —including procedures and policies. First, he established his *objectives:* to lose twenty-five pounds, and then to maintain his weight at the new level. The *plan* was to write down every food and beverage item he consumed and the number of calories contained in each. He did this every time he put something in his mouth, and kept a running account of his caloric intake. This act made him conscious of how much he was actually eating each time he ingested something, and it reminded him how much he had eaten prior to that. He determined that according to his height and frame he should limit his daily intake to two thousand calories.

In addition to following this procedure on a daily basis, he also established some eating *policies* which he followed. He refused to eat pastries and ice cream or drink alcoholic beverages. These are high-calorie foods; if he ate or drank them he would quickly use up his caloric allotment for the day. He felt he could not afford to do that. Another policy he adopted was that when he became hungry he would eat or drink a low-calorie item; fruits, water, and raw vegetables took the place of peanuts, cookies, and other high-calorie goodies.

Within three months he reached his weight-loss goal. In order to maintain his weight, he continued to honor his policies. He also thought about what he ate. While he no longer had to keep his notebook, he had established a new habit pattern of eating. As of this writing, he has not deviated more than a couple of pounds.

The test of effective planning is whether or not the plan leads you to action and moves you forward. If it does not, the plan has to be reevaluated and changed. But you have to take some action. Plans are meaningless unless they trigger positive activity. In a job, if you do not implement established plans, you are called on the carpet and eventually fired if you don't shape up. The rewards for following through on your commitment are a paycheck, personal satisfaction, and possible raises or promotions.

In the business of living the penalty for not implementing your plans is continual disappointment and stagnancy. Your potential rewards are 100 per cent profit. You always win when you fulfill your promises to yourself, because *you* reap all the benefits. Can you afford to pass up such a deal?

8

The Best Kind of Discipline

"Sure," you say, "it's easy to tell myself that I'm going to do something. I may even develop plans for accomplishing my objectives. But how do I make myself do those things that have to be done?"

The question of self-discipline plagues many people. There is no magical solution to the problem of overcoming physical and intellectual inertia. Even knowing that you are your own boss, and that *you* will capitalize on your achievements, doesn't help too much. It is easier to let things slide and to put things off, even though the price of procrastination and lack of initiative is great. Nevertheless, the fact is that if you want to be an effective manager of your business you must *learn to motivate yourself,* rather than relying on others to push you. But how?

Getting into a productive frame of mind is probably the first step. This I learned from a woman who was an educational and vocational counselor when I was head of that department at the Rehabilitation Institute of Chicago, a hospital that helps people develop the skills they need to function or cope with their physical disabilities.

Irene was, and still is, a quadriplegic—a victim of an automobile accident that left her paralyzed from the neck down. Her hands and arms were the only parts of her body that still had some life. Irene struggled long and hard to reach the level of independence she had already achieved by the time I met her.

71

After undergoing the complex medical treatment normally required with such a disability, she enrolled in graduate school and received a master's degree in counseling. She later learned how to drive a car equipped especially for her; she also maintained her own apartment. All this she accomplished while confined to a wheelchair.

Irene was, and still is, a beautiful and highly productive person. Her smile was infectious. She also got more things done, despite her limitations, than did most able-bodied people I knew. She wrote, read, cooked, and even found time to attend lectures, concerts, and entertain guests. Later, I found out, she pursued a doctoral program and received her degree.

One day I asked Irene, "What is your secret? How do you, in your condition, accomplish so many things?" I shall never forget her response.

She drew a large square with a small circle inside it on a blank piece of paper. "You see this big square?" she asked. "That's your world. The small circle is you. Because you are so small compared to the world around you, you are subject to all kinds of distractions. You also have an unlimited capacity to flit from one activity to another. There is nothing to hold you back. If you're reading, and you feel like going out, you go out. If someone calls you while you're doing something, and asks you to go somewhere, you have a choice. The point is, because of your mobility you have many options available to you, all of which compete for your attention."

Then she took another sheet of blank paper and drew a very small square with a large circle inside, which took up practically the entire space. "That," she said, "represents my situation. As you can see, I don't have too many choices. Once I have committed myself to doing what I want to do or what has to be done, that's it. It's just too great a problem to shift gears and be tempted by another activity. I can't even consider anything else. So, I just settle into my wheelchair and make up my mind to finish what I start. It's too physically tiring to give in to distractions, so I don't."

Does Irene's explanation have value for those of us who are not physically disabled? I would say it does. Every time I have to do something that requires concentration or undivided attention I think of Irene. "Pretend," I say to myself, "that you are confined to this place or project, and that there is nothing you can do about it until you've completed what you've set out to do. Consider yourself immobile until you've fulfilled your promise to yourself." Within a relatively short time I am able to shut out the rest of the world and set myself to accomplishing whatever goal I have established. As contrived and artificial as this method may seem, it works for me.

Is it any different from the techniques managers use in business? Why is it that when a boss sets a deadline for completing a particular project, we seem to find the time and energy to do it? Because *a deadline imposes a pressure that gives us the impetus to complete the project.* Under these conditions we are able to insulate ourselves from and disregard distractions that deter us from our course. If we can do it when others create the pressure, we can certainly do it by creating our own limited amount of pressure.

That's what is meant by *self-discipline.* It is *training yourself to accomplish those daily and weekly objectives you set for yourself.* Discipline is not, as many people believe, punishment. When an effective manager disciplines a subordinate, his intention is to teach that employee to abide by the company's standards, policies, and procedures. When parents discipline a child, they attempt to train the youngster to behave in a manner that is acceptable to them. While punishment may be employed as part of the training, it need not be.

Similarly, when you exercise self-discipline, you are in effect putting into practice techniques that help you attend to those things that must get done. The self-disciplined person has trained himself to fulfill his obligations to himself and others.

There are no specific self-disciplining techniques that work for everyone; we all have to find our own. Let me suggest several:

1. As I said earlier, one of the methods that work for me is

pretending that I am restricted from doing anything else until I have completed what I promised myself to do.

2. Another technique that many people employ effectively is to *write down the things they must get done today.* This daily "things-to-do list," which may be compiled every morning, serves as a constant reminder of what has to be accomplished on a particular day. One of the benefits of such a list is the satisfaction that comes from scratching out things as they are done.

One man I know writes at the top of the list, "Eat breakfast." His reason? It assures him that he will at least have one item scratched off. A things-to-do list also reduces the "I've got so much on my mind" feeling many busy people are prone to.

To make this list truly effective, you might consider noting the amount of time you want to devote to a particular activity. This will serve as a commitment to yourself. It says, in effect, "Don't stop doing whatever you're involved in until you've put in this designated amount of time." To help you stick with the commitment you might offer yourself a reward *after* you have invested the time you said you would. Your reward may be anything that is personally meaningful to you.

3. Still another way of disciplining yourself is to *think about the positive results you will achieve when you are finished.* This is a particularly useful technique when you are doing things you view as drudgery. A bachelor friend of mine who absolutely despises cleaning his apartment told me that when cleaning time comes around he tries to visualize what the apartment will look like after the job is completed. This, he says, serves as an incentive to get started.

Getting started is almost always difficult, especially when you have to do things you don't like or when the things you must do require great effort. I don't know of any simple way of reducing this difficulty. What all these techniques boil down to is this: You have to sell yourself on the value of doing what needs to be done. Having done a good selling job, you have taken the most important step toward action.

9

When Things Go Wrong

Murphy's Law states that if anything can go wrong it will. Adversity and problems are ever present, or lurking around the corner. Whether we are talking about the business of living or commercial enterprises, people frequently face real or imagined obstacles that stand between them and their desired objectives. Things *do* go wrong, even with the best-laid plans. We *do* have limitations and weaknesses that may prevent us from doing all we would like. Our environment and the people we associate with are not all that predictable.

Faced with a difficulty, the initial question you must answer is, "Do I give in to these problems and allow them to overwhelm me, or do I cope with them in some constructive way?"

Let's look at some of the ways people deal with problems. We'll begin with what are usually less than successful means, and work our way toward what seems a more productive approach.

1. Take the case of Carl, who claimed that he was looking for a new job. "There isn't a job around," he said. "Every time I investigate a position that looks interesting, it's filled."

"How are you going about looking for a job?" I asked, suspecting that he was doing something wrong.

"Well, I look in the Sunday paper. And, when I see something that appeals to me, I cut out the ad."

"What do you do next?"

"I can't check on it on Monday and Tuesday because those

are busy days for me. So, on Wednesday I make my calls. But by that time the jobs are taken."

No one could argue with Carl that he tried. But his efforts were meager and his expectations were unrealistic. Of course there were no opportunities available—not the way he went about exploring them.

Hoping or wishing for things to happen, spinning your wheels and going nowhere, or complaining vehemently about your plight is futile. These actions are about as effective as using a soup ladle to bail out a sinking boat.

I have seen people throw up their hands in disgust when their actions produce no results. But they delude themselves *because what they do is guaranteed to produce failure.*

2. Another way of responding to problems is to *assume you are basically unable to cope.* People who browbeat themselves and assume a self-deprecating attitude do so to diminish their feelings of guilt for not taking constructive action. It is their way of paying their "dues" for their mistakes, failure, or inactivity.

By announcing to the world that they are inadequate, sick, or unambitious they can get others to feel sorry for them. In their own minds such pronouncements also relieve their responsibility to themselves and others. "After all," they reason, "if I'm incapable, how can anyone expect me to produce?" For these people breast-beating takes the place of problem-solving. But it doesn't get them anywhere.

3. Some people have discovered a third technique for handling problems—what are called *ego-defensive reactions,* or responses that serve to protect them from attacks, either from themselves or from others. All of us use them to one degree or another. When employed in moderation, they are useful. However, when they are overused, they are unhealthy. Why?

In the business of living, people frequently deceive themselves with ego defenses, which become excuses and cover-ups for not acting in a responsible and mature manner. Normally, we do not realize when we are being defensive; that's one of the advantages of this method. Nobody likes to admit he is fooling himself.

I believe you can reduce the frequency with which you use this technique by being aware of what it involves and how people use it. Let us look at three of the more common and perhaps most destructive "defenses"—rationalization, projection, and denial:

Rationalization. This is probably one of the most frequently used defenses. Rationalizations reduce our disappointment when we can't get what we want; they also help us to justify those actions and beliefs that are not acceptable to others. One form of rationalization is "sour grapes." This is based on the Aesop fable of the fox who very much wanted the delicious-looking grapes he spotted on a tree. After several unsuccessful attempts to get the grapes, he said: "I don't really want them, they're probably sour."

Nowhere in the fable does it say that the fox tried to look for a box or ladder on which he could climb to extend his reach. Nor does it mention anything about his making a deal to share the grapes with another animal if he could climb on its back to get at the fruit. Instead he excused his failure by denying his desire and deciding that he didn't really want the grapes after all.

The fox was probably better off excusing himself that way than he would have been thinking himself a dumb and inadequate animal who would never amount to anything. But his rationalization was not as productive as saying to himself, "I really want those grapes. And even though I can't have them now, I will keep an eye open for the help I need to reach them."

You would be surprised at how many opportunities people miss out on, and all the problems people fail to resolve, because of this type of rationalization. Personal growth is impeded when you deny your desires or interests just because you encounter an obstacle. If you focus your thinking on how you can achieve a particular desire, rather than on fooling yourself into believing that what you want is not that important, you just might find a way of accomplishing your objectives.

Another form of rationalization is to justify behavior others may not approve of. One day, strictly for my own amusement, I decided to count the number of times people used this tactic in handling their problems. In just a single day I was able to spot the use of this kind of rationalization ten different times. Here are just a few incidents in which it came up, and the exact statements that were used.

A professor's explanation for why he was not writing articles for publication: "Being a devoted family man, I don't want to take time away from my wife and children. If I devoted time to writing I wouldn't be as good a family man as I'd like to be."

A student's reasoning for doing poorly on an exam: "Nobody really cares what grades I get as long as I get my degree."

A husband explaining to his wife why he cheated on her: "I felt that if I got it out of my system, I would appreciate you more."

And finally, a salesman who was earning a modest salary because he did not work diligently at his job: "What's the sense of knocking yourself out? The government gets most of your money anyway."

These self-deceptions and illogical explanations are probably effective protectors of these people's egos. But they are useless as far as uncovering and doing something about the true causes of their behavior is concerned. Individuals who become accustomed to fooling themselves in this way rarely accomplish anything. They are so busy trying to explain their weaknesses and failures that they fail to take the necessary time to understand their *real* motives and thereby solve their dilemma in a mature and realistic manner.

Projection. "The devil made me do it," "Everyone else cheats, why shouldn't I?" "They don't promote Jews [Catholics, Protestants, blacks, women, etc.]," "Luck is not on my side." These are all projections. People who employ this defensive tactic find solace in blaming others for their misfortunes. It is as if they are saying, "I am not responsible for what I do. My judgments and skills have nothing to do with the way I conduct my life."

To these people I say: "If you want to hit a dog, you can always find a stick. You can always find someone or something on which you can project your shortcomings. You can always blame conditions and circumstances for not obtaining what you want, or for not doing things you know are in your best interest."

Finding fault with others, and charging people and things with the responsibility for creating your problems, may get you off the hook for the moment; when you are looking for a dog to hit you don't have to think about yourself and your responsibilities. But what does it do to advance your business? Nothing.

When this temptation arises, you might find it helpful to ask yourself, "Does blaming someone else have a constructive value, aside from making me feel better?" If your answer to this question is no, you are then ready to ask yourself the next question, "What am *I* going to do about my problem?" Having accepted the responsibility of facing up to your weaknesses and difficulties, you are on your way toward effective resolutions.

Denial. Another unhealthy defensive tactic is to ignore your problem and bury your head in the sand. When a person denies that a problem exists he doesn't have to do anything about it. But the fact of the matter is that unpleasant situations or difficulties do not vanish just because we don't think about them. Rather, such a defense might compound the problem.

One man I knew casually mentioned to his wife that he was having chest pains. When she urged him to go to the doctor he assured her that it was nothing—just gas. On one occasion he became terribly pale and weak, and had to lie down. When his wife wanted to get medical help, he instructed her not to; he reiterated his conviction that it was nothing to get alarmed about. Several weeks later he suffered a severe heart attack and had to be hospitalized. As it turned out, he had had several attacks prior to that which he chose to ignore. By ignoring them he made his condition worse.

Denying unpleasant reality is like sweeping dirt under the carpet. The garbage is there whether or not you acknowledge it. Some people fail to face up to reality because they don't know how to handle it—they're not certain what they would do, even if they accepted a particular fact. So they wait until they are forced to act.

These are individuals who, when you ask them, "What's wrong?" because from all appearances something *is*, will say, "Nothing." If you try to get at the truth, they'll get angry with you. What they don't realize is that by not admitting to their problems, either to themselves or to those they trust, they can't take appropriate steps to resolve them.

Denial of reality is commonly referred to as escapism. The tactic here is, if you're not emotionally ready to face a problem, run away from it. The executive who regularly works sixteen hours a day to avoid his domestic problems, for example, denies that he is escaping from his home responsibilities, and rationalizes his behavior by saying that he is too busy earning a living.

The person who keeps putting off things he doesn't enjoy but must get done is another case in point. So is the housewife who runs from one social or community activity to another while ignoring her own household and motherly responsibilities. I'm not saying that social or community involvements are wrong, if this is a conscious choice. But as escape measures they are defensive in nature.

To repeat a statement I made earlier: Ego defenses have their place and value. But they cannot replace constructive steps for dealing with problems, frustrations, or tensions.

4. "All right," you say, "now I know what *not* to do when things go wrong. What should I do instead?" My answer: *You can deal with them realistically*. If you took this position, you would consider *every possible route* available to you for overcoming those obstacles or weaknesses which are causing you

difficulties. You would then take whatever positive actions you could to *remove the barrier*. You may need help from others, but that's better than giving up before you have exhausted all avenues.

I learned this lesson in a dramatic and painful way a number of years ago. At the time, I was working for a market-research firm that conducted studies of attitudes toward consumer products. After we had written a comprehensive report on a survey in which I was involved, the client asked us to give an oral presentation of our findings to the client's top executives and their advertising agency's marketing group.

I had never given an oral presentation before, nor had I ever talked before a large group of people. But my boss felt I could do the job, so I accepted the invitation to represent our firm.

My nervousness and lack of experience was evident as I oh'd and um'd and ah'd through my entire presentation. It was clear that I was "bombing"; the high-level group I was addressing was fidgety and seemingly uncomfortable. They were obviously not getting their money's worth, and I knew it. As I stumbled my way through to the last flip chart, it became clear that the whole experience was a disaster. Nobody even talked to me after I was finished.

On the plane back to Chicago I sat next to the agency's vice-president for marketing. He said, "You know you made a fool of yourself and us too, don't you?" I nodded. "And you know you will never do any work for us again, don't you?" I nodded again. "But," he continued, "you can go home and feel sorry for yourself, and even get drunk if you like. Or you can do something about your inability to talk before a group."

"What do you suggest?" I asked.

"Take a speech course or join the Toastmasters Club," he said. "It's not going to change what happened, but hopefully you'll be better prepared next time you're in a similar situation."

The next day, after a terribly restless night's sleep, I took his advice and inquired about joining a local Toastmasters Club. It was hard work learning to overcome my fear of talking before an audience. But I kept at it. Three months later I won my first "best speaker" award.

Suppose, you might ask, a person tries every possible way to solve his problem, but without success? Under those conditions a realistic solution is to accept the fact that what you want is not within your grasp. Gracefully accepting your limitations when you have done all you could to overcome them, and directing your energies to another project, is certainly a realistic way of handling a problem.

Your business of living cannot thrive unless you are honest with yourself and the difficulties that face you. When possible, search for the *real* explanations for your behavior; it's the only place to begin building the kind of business you really want.

Part 3

GETTING OTHERS
TO WORK WITH YOU

10

No Person Is an Island

A cartoon I once saw pictured two people leaning on each other. The caption read: "We need each other for support." So it is with all of us. While we are proprietors of our own business, we need to interact with others. We need to work with people; we need their cooperation; we need their emotional support. In short, *we need people as emotional, intellectual, and financial resources to help us* in the business of living.

Similarly, any company's most important assets are its people. To enhance the productive value of these assets, an organization's top executives must create a cooperative working climate. This can be accomplished by communicating effectively with the people who work with and for them, and by encouraging their associates and subordinates to do the same. Building good people relations throughout an entire organization is the best investment a company can make toward achieving its long- and short-range goals.

This philosophy also holds true in the business of living. Your attitudes, as reflected in your words and actions, influence other people's reaction toward you. To improve your personal relations skills is a two-stage process. First, you must critically *examine what you do or don't do that turns people either off or on.* Having this knowledge of yourself, you will be prepared for the second step: to *alter the behavior and attitudes that need changing.*

You can do much to create a favorable communication climate, and to get people to work with you instead of against you. By employing some of the principles discussed in this chapter you will increase your awareness of yourself and your sensitivity toward other people. You will also reduce the degree to which others misinterpret you.

Back Up Your Words with Action

It's ironic: while words are our main method for communicating with each other, they are not particularly dependable tools. Words alone can be, and often are, deceptive. People say many things that they don't really mean, or that may have a variety of meanings. For example, an acquaintance may say, "Let's get together sometime." Does that person mean "I enjoy your company, and would like to see you again?" Or is this statement a friendly parting comment which has no other significance? Similarly, your boss may say, "You're doing a nice job." It could well be a sincere compliment, or it might mean "If I give him a bone, he'll be content and stay off my back."

As a result of many disappointing experiences, we have learned to doubt, or at least question, the sincerity of other people's words. Take this situation, for example: Someone says to you, "Call on me if I can be of any assistance to you." So, when a problem arises requiring that person's help you call him, but he is too busy and suggests you try him again. Accepting his invitation, you phone him several more times. Unable to get through to him, you leave messages to return your call. You get no response. What are you to think? Did he extend the offer because it was what he felt *you* wanted to hear? Did he really mean what he said?

Is it any wonder you and I place relatively little value on what people say? Not if you've been on the receiving end of words that lack substance and are not backed up with appropriate action. Credibility gaps are common in our society. Many advertisers make claims not supported by facts; politicians frequently fail to deliver on their promises; academicians often teach principles they themselves don't practice. When the actions of a person belie his words, your confidence in that individual has to diminish.

While lack of credibility is a social problem, you do not have to perpetuate it in your own business of living. You can reduce the extent to which people doubt or misinterpret your words if you take into consideration two factors. First, all of us are insecure to some degree. Nobody is completely sure of himself, or of others, in every situation. Consequently, people need all the concrete evidence you can present to convince them of your sincerity. They need all the assurance you can offer that what you say is what you mean.

Words alone stimulate people's visual or auditory sense, depending upon whether they read or hear your words. To be convincing, you must stimulate other parts of their physical and emotional makeup. They need to *feel* what you say. They want to be *shown* that your words are meaningful, not mere rhetoric. Perhaps this is why telephone conversations can be frustrating; neither party can *see* what the other is saying.

You can make your words more credible if you put into practice the principle that actions speak louder than words. *Promise only what you can deliver.* If, for some reason, you can't fulfill a promise, let the other person know so he's not left hanging. When you compliment people do it with sincere enthusiasm; pat them on the back to show you care. Don't talk about what you're going to do; *do it.*

Credibility gaps also are created when your words do not reflect your actions. You may be angry at someone, and demonstrate your feelings by pouting, throwing things around, or perhaps not talking to the individual. So he asks you, "What's wrong?" or "Are you angry with me?" If you respond, with teeth clenched, of course, "Nothing's wrong," he's confused. Your actions say one thing, your words say something else. What is he to believe? You would be doing yourself and him greater justice if you said, "Of course I'm angry." At least then you have a basis for discussing what's bothering you.

Following through on your words with appropriate actions and reinforcing your actions with descriptive words are vital principles for maintaining honest communications. They also tie in closely with other principles of effective personal relations, still to be discussed.

Assumptions Are Not Facts

The kinds of assumptions we make about people influence our actions toward them. If you assume a particular individual is decent and honest and would not intentionally hurt you, your actions toward that person will reflect these feelings. On the other hand, if you assume a person is malicious, jealous, selfish, spiteful, or dishonest, chances are you will be on guard and weigh every word you say.

Admittedly we have to make some assumptions about the world we live in and the people we associate with. For example, you go to work every day and perform your job because you assume you will receive a paycheck at the end of a working period. You also assume that your failure to meet the demands of your job, whether you work at home or travel to your place of employment, will produce unfavorable consequences. Going on past experiences, we are confident these assumptions are reasonable.

Since assumptions are nothing more than beliefs, speculations, and possibilities, they may or may not prove to be correct. Unfortunately, however, we frequently make false assumptions (although we don't know they are false), but we act as if they were true. This is commonly referred to as "jumping to conclusions." Treating assumptions as if they were facts is being unfair to others as well as to yourself. It can also be embarrassing, as I discovered several years ago.

While shopping in a local department store, I met a former neighbor whom I had not seen in years. "How are you?" I asked.

"I guess you haven't heard. Bill and I just went through a divorce."

Showing obvious concern for what I assumed was a sad event, I said: "Gee, I'm terribly sorry."

"Not me," she replied. "I was glad to get rid of him. Living with Bill was pure hell. And now that it's over with I feel like a human being again."

Taken aback by her reaction, all I could say was, "Well, I'm delighted for you."

This experience taught me a valuable lesson. Since then, when anyone informs me about his or her divorce, I first ask, "Are condolences or congratulations in order?" Depending upon what they say, I respond with whatever comments seem appropriate.

Embarrassments like this are mild compared to other possible consequences of acting on erroneous assumptions. Sometimes they can even destroy relationships. A conscientious and dedicated machinist I know was ostracized by several of his work friends. They assumed he was trying to make the other workers "look bad" when he refused to take longer coffee breaks than the company allowed. He also insisted on producing his best, rather than going along with the low production standards maintained by other department members. The assumption of his co-workers was wrong: his intention was not to hurt them, but rather to uphold his own professional values.

Many people assume the worst of others. If a friend hasn't called in several weeks he "must be angry." If a neighbor buys a new car, he's "showing off" or "putting on the dog." If a business associate refuses a luncheon or dinner invitation, he "doesn't like me." These negative assumptions fail to consider the possibility that *other people's actions are not necessarily directed at you personally.* You could just as easily assume that circumstances and other factors having nothing at all to do with you influence their actions and decisions.

A more complicated variation of this tendency to act on false assumptions occurs when a person carries on a two-way conversation with himself. This process is dramatically illustrated in an incident related to me by a former patient.

Harry was angry and upset because he had not received a raise for what seemed to him to be a long time. He was firmly convinced that he had been deliberately passed up. Thinking about the problem, he weighed the pros and cons of approaching his boss about his concern. "Chances are," he thought, "if I ask him I'll be turned down anyway. Why would he do that? He must be unhappy with my work. But he has no reason to be displeased. If that's all he thinks of me I better look for another job," he concluded.

His reasoning prompted him to march into his superior's office with his announcement: "I quit."

Shocked, the boss insisted on discussing Harry's seemingly irrational decision. "Frankly, it was an oversight. Why didn't you come in to talk to me earlier?" the boss asked.

"Well," Harry replied, "I was sure you passed me up for a raise because you were unhappy with my work. And since you felt that way, I figured that I better find a new job."

Harry literally talked himself into believing he was not wanted. He imputed intentions, attitudes, and feelings to his boss that were not based on facts, but he acted as if they were. Harry's decision to quit resulted from his imagined conversation between himself and his boss. His indictments and accusations, which resulted in an impulsive action, stemmed from his failure to check out his initial assumption—that he was deliberately passed up for a raise.

Harry's problem is fairly common. People frequently talk to and answer themselves. They silently make comments to themselves and they raise questions about another person's motives. Then they respond to these comments and answer their own questions (for the other person, of course). If they don't like the answers or comments they imagine the other person gives them, they become increasingly angry until they react, and usually their reactions are inappropriate or unreasonable.

This process is what I call "mental masturbation," for the feedback you receive is limited to what you yourself feel and believe. When you answer your own questions about issues and problems that require input from other people, you are not getting the information you need to make good judgments.

Mental masturbation is destructive because you do not give the other person a chance to respond to your concerns and questions. In effect, you become a hanging jury of one. You not only hang yourself, because you talk yourself into problems with people when there may not be any, but you also create barriers toward resolving differences. Nobody likes to be wrongly accused of intentions, thoughts, or actions.

Occasionally, and perhaps without realizing it, we create conditions where we stimulate people to mentally masturbate. Consider this incident which happened to one of my graduate students: One Friday afternoon at 4:45 his boss phoned him. "Joe, I want to see you first thing Monday morning." He then hung up.

Poor Joe was a basket case over the weekend. He imagined all kinds of things. At first he wondered what he had done wrong. The more he thought, the more angry he became. He honestly believed he was doing a good job, and, if his boss had a complaint, it was unwarranted.

By Monday he had an obvious chip on his shoulder. He was all set for a battle. Joe's boss, after the usual greeting, told him that his reason for wanting this meeting was to discuss his outstanding performance, and that he was being rewarded with a promotion. All of Joe's anguish could have been prevented with a simple explanation on Friday. Furthermore, Joe could have waited until Monday; he did not need to engage in unhealthy mental gymnastics to the point of ruining his weekend.

How can you overcome the problem of making and acting on

erroneous assumptions? How can you avoid falsely accusing others of intentions to hurt, disappoint, or discredit you? I have several suggestions:

Verify your assumptions. You can, for example, state your attitudes or feelings as a belief rather than a fact: "I assume you didn't call me because something came up." Or, you might present your attitudes in the form of a question: "I hope you didn't *mean* to embarrass me when you made that comment?" When possible, give the other person the benefit of the doubt. Until you have evidence to the contrary, you are better off to assume a person's intentions are not deliberate attempts to upset you.

Even if you present your assumptions in negative terms—for example, "I *suppose* you really intended to make me look foolish"—you still leave the door open for discussion. The other person has an opportunity to agree with, correct, or refute your assumptions. Regardless of whether your assumptions are positively or negatively stated, the result is the same: you are not making false accusations.

Suppose the other person is not honest in responding to your statements or questions? Frankly, it doesn't matter, because you still will have made your feelings and attitudes known. However, you have done it in a way which would not close the doors to effective communication. Furthermore, if you like you can elaborate on your feelings without turning off the other person. You might say: "I assume you have good reason for not being at the meeting. But I was disappointed that you weren't there."

One final point: There are times when you are not able to state your assumptions directly to the person who disappointed you. Even then, for your own mental health, and assuming he doesn't take advantage of your good nature too often, you would feel better if you told yourself, "I suppose he has his reasons." Holding grudges does nobody any good.

Respect Is a Two-way Street

Effective managers are able to command respect from those people who work with and for them. They are also willing to extend to others the respect they rightly deserve. I believe these two qualities—ability to command respect and willingness to offer it—are related. You can't expect to receive respect unless you give it. Respect for others, as well as for yourself, is a vital requirement for developing good interpersonal relations.

Literally, the term "respect" means to look at *(spect)* again *(re)*. When you look at someone again, as opposed to ignoring the individual, you are giving that person a second thought. Rather than disregarding him, you perceive him as a unique human being whose ideas and feelings are important; he is worthy of whatever time and attention you can give him. To show respect for another person you must seriously consider what he is saying, doing, or feeling.

A basic requirement for demonstrating respect toward people you associate with is to *be sensitive to their needs.* But what, you might ask, are their needs, and aren't they different for every person? Frankly, other people's major personal needs are no different from yours and mine. We all need to be listened to, and to have our distinctive human qualities recognized or acknowledged. Nobody likes to be taken for granted or to go unnoticed. People resent being ignored. We do not like it when others do not care about what we do or say.

Sensitivity toward others can be developed. But first you must accept one important fact: *Every person lives in his own private world. The way others view and react to people and their experiences is based upon their individual physiological states, their upbringing, and their unique psychological makeup.* Once you recognize this truth you will be more receptive to what others do and say. You will be more inclined to listen to them and to find out how they perceive the world around them. You will not be so quick to judge others on the basis of how *you* would react to a given situation. Rather, you will attempt to determine where others "live," both emotionally and intellectually.

To develop respect for others, you have to get into their shoes and to recognize that their feelings are as important to them as yours are to you. You exhibit respect for another person when you show your concern for his emotional state, and when you acknowledge that person's point of view. This does not mean you have to agree with those you respect, nor does it mean you must share their feelings. Just acknowledge their existence and human worth. Comments like "I can appreciate what you're going through" show you care.

Unfortunately, many people are too preoccupied with their own world, with their intellectual and emotional "sales kits," to listen to others. Here again we might take a tip from business: The primary job of an effective salesperson is to respect the customer's problems, and address himself to his concerns. Once he finds out where his customer is at, and what his needs are, he will know how to appeal to his customer with the products he has available. Knowledge of the customer's world and his perceptions of it can give a salesperson many clues for becoming more effective.

What is to be gained from respecting others? Aside from the benefits I've already mentioned, you gain important information that may be useful to you. A highly successful manager I know explained: "I can't afford not to respect the people I work with. I never know what they might teach me, nor can I predict what ideas they might come up with which could benefit me by helping me do my job better. I don't necessarily follow every thought they present, but at least I give them the opportunity to voice their views, which I later think about."

Admittedly, you can't respect each person for everything he says or does. For example, you would obviously pay more attention to what a stockbroker might say about the market than you would to a local bartender. Similarly, while you might listen to your neighbor about how she might handle a particular illness you have, you would not respect her advice as much as you would your physician's. Your good judgment would dictate what subjects you can broach with whom, and how much credence you can give to each person.

When you extend respect to others you are in effect assuming that every individual has something worthwhile to convey to you, be they feelings, attitudes, or ideas. And, until he proves otherwise, he has a right to be heard. You also owe it to yourself to determine whether you can learn something from that person. You always have the option to filter out the relevant from the irrelevant, or to turn him off when you realize he has nothing significant to offer you. But you can't accurately predict who is or is not worthy of serious consideration until you listen.

Frankly, I have learned a great deal from cab drivers, gas station attendants, store clerks, and students, as well as from my own children. Why? Because I want to know what they feel and think about various issues of mutual interest. If I were to ignore them because they were less educated or younger than me, I hate to think what I would miss.

A personal philosophy that continues to guide my behavior toward others, and one which I try to teach is this: We all have one thing in common—each of us is a human being. If we can't listen and be sensitive to each other we are all in trouble.

Respect is infectious; when you extend it others tend to reciprocate. And when others listen to you and give you a second thought, you develop self-confidence. In the process you develop greater respect for yourself, and the value you place on your thoughts, feelings, and attitudes increases. The net result is that everyone wins.

Developing Trust in Others

Trust, like respect, is an essential ingredient for developing effective personal relations. There are at least three components of trust. First, I can trust you if I feel assured you will fulfill your obligations and promises to me. Second, I can trust you if I feel certain you will not misuse, undermine, or misjudge whatever emotions, ideas, or personal facts I share with you. And finally, I can trust you if I feel confident you will accept or try to understand any weaknesses or shortcomings I reveal to you, rather than using them as weapons to hurt me.

I've never known anyone who completely fulfills these criteria. Since we are complex human beings, our filtering mechanism is not predictable. We rarely know for certain how others will take what we say. So whenever we share information or feelings with others, or even ask questions, we take risks. We may be judged wrongly or be reprimanded; we may even offend others inadvertently. Our reluctance to communicate honestly with others is based, in part, on our fears of these consequences.

Even compliments can sometimes be taken in the wrong way. How often have you asked yourself, when someone offered you a compliment, "Is he sincere or is he trying to butter me up?" "Does she really mean what she says, or is she just trying to be nice?" In short, "Can I trust what this person says?" Obviously, if you have had these thoughts, so have others.

If even simple compliments can be misinterpreted, it is understandable that many people are reluctant, if not defensive, when communicating with others. Your willingness to take the risks involved in relating to someone depends upon how well you know a person, and your assessment of the potential dangers.

If you've ever seen two animals fighting you know what I mean by potential dangers. Typically, they begin by circling each other, carefully assessing their opponent. Then, at just the right moment, each animal lunges toward the other. Both attack their adversary's vulnerable area. Once an animal draws blood, he attacks the bruised spot more forcefully and deliberately. His attack continues until the opponent runs away or is subdued.

People also have a tendency to look for and attack the weaknesses of those they view as enemies, when it suits their purposes. But their approach is more sophisticated. Instead of throwing jabs that hurt physically, their attacks are verbal and the pain created is emotional. With a word or action—ignoring someone, violating a person's confidence, or misinterpreting an individual's motives—we can cause "internal bleeding."

Recognizing our human frailties, the question we have to deal with is, How can we develop a more accurate filtering device so we minimize the risk of trusting others too much or too little? To put the question differently: How do we develop the judgment to know how much to say, and to whom?

In business a boss develops trust in a subordinate by initially giving him a small project or assignment to do. If he handles it well, the superior increases the complexity of the next project. And so it goes. The boss determines the degree of trust he can have in his subordinates by how effectively they perform their assignment. You can determine for yourself the type and extent of trust you can have in people you deal with by similar means.

Let us say you have a friend or acquaintance whom you would like to trust, but you don't know if you can. Share a bit of innocuous information with that person. Or let him know how you feel about a particular issue. How does he handle your comments? Does he judge or accept them? Does he tell you how to run your life or does he respect your individuality? The outcome of this test will tell you something about this person. You can test him for his dependability, honesty, sensitivity, helpfulness, or any other quality you're interested in.

By employing tests like these you will, in time, be able to determine the degree of trust you can place in this person. What you are searching for is boundaries. Having discovered these boundaries, or limits, you will sharpen your judgment of what you can or can't expect from this person. Hopefully, you will know that if you overstep these limits you are certain to be disappointed.

By testing and discovering the limitations of your friends and associates—and we all do it—you will be able to accept them for what they are. You will not ask anything of them that you know they can't deliver. Nor will you share confidences with them you know they can't keep. You will have a relationship on a level they can handle, and on a basis you can live with.

But remember: you, too, may be tested.

The Importance of Timing

All of us have days when things go wrong. A bad start in the morning, an unpleasant encounter, or a bit of bad news can create an emotional state which may cause us to fly off the handle regardless of what is said or who says it. A person in this state may well take out his feelings on you if you're nearby. His blow-up may have nothing to do with you. You just happened to be in the wrong place at the wrong time.

Of course you have no way of knowing in advance when this might happen. But if you are ever the object of a tirade or a rebuff, you might ask yourself: "Is it me, or did I approach him at a bad time?" Don't automatically assume the person you are talking with is reacting to you personally. You might even ask the other person, "Is this a bad time to discuss this?" Chances are he'll tell you.

Many people inadvertently subject themselves to negative reactions or refusals to their requests because their timing is poor. An employee who approaches his boss for a raise just as the boss is getting ready for a meeting is a case in point. Obviously the employee is going to be rejected or he will receive some short comment which can easily be misinterpreted.

From time to time students stop me in the hall, as I'm on my way to a class, to discuss their grades. Their apparent lack of concern for my rush causes me to respond gruffly, "Not now," as I walk away from them. Naturally, they feel hurt because I fail to respect their desires. Similarly, people have told me how offended they get when they phone a business associate to talk about something or other, and they get a quick brush-off.

In each of these examples the person making the approach—the employee, student, and caller—assumes that just because he is eager to talk about a problem the other person should be also. That assumption is obviously unfounded. What is important to you at this moment need not necessarily be of concern to someone else. So, if you approach a person with a problem at a time when he is not ready to talk about it, you're taking a chance on a bad response.

You can increase your chances of being received favorably by others if you respect their time. When you call someone, ask: "Do you have a few minutes to talk?" or "I'd like to talk to you about such and such. Do you have a few minutes or would you rather I call back at a more convenient time?" The point is if what you want to talk to a person about is important, you want his undivided attention. If you settle for less than that, you are shortchanging yourself.

I'm sure the boss in our example would have preferred if the employee had called and said: "I'd like to make an appointment to see you." In the case of students, I am quite receptive when they ask to see me at a time that is mutually convenient. When they do, I am emotionally and intellectually ready to engage in any discussion of interest to them.

In short, you have to appreciate that others have their own set of priorities, and that you don't automatically become number one because you want it that way.

Your Tone of Voice Gives You Away

Few people think about their tone of voice. Yet most of us have been on either the receiving or the giving end of the admonishment, "I don't like your tone of voice." When confronted with this criticism, most people act surprised. A typical retort is, "What's wrong with my tone of voice?" To which the critic responds, "I don't know, but I don't like it." What a dilemma.

How do you correct a behavior which can only be described as unpleasant or offensive?

It can be done. Before I offer a workable solution, let's look at what your voice tells people. *Regardless of the words you employ, your tone of voice conveys your attitude toward others.* You can sound sarcastic or sincere, happy or sad, enthusiastic or bored, interested or uninvolved, angry or sympathetic. Since people respond to your tone of voice, as well as to your words, how you say things is just as important as what you say.

For our first example, let's assume I come to my office wearing a pair of slacks, a sport shirt, and a sweater. And one of my patients says: "You're not dressed like a professional." My response might be, "What do you mean, I'm not dressed like a professional?" Depending upon my tone of voice, I could convey one of two meanings: How dare you criticize the way I dress? Or, Would you explain what, in your opinion, is appropriate attire for a professional?

Similarly, suppose a person requests that you do something; you might respond by saying: "Sure, I'll do it." Again, depending upon your tone of voice, your statement could express one of two attitudes: "Yes, I'll be happy to," or "I'll do it, but I don't want to." Even simple factual information could be conveyed in a way that says: "Here's some information that might interest you," or "Here's some information you should have known about. How dumb can you be not to have heard of it before?" In each of the above examples one tone of voice transmits an offensive attitude and places the other person on the defensive, while the other tone imparts a desire to know or to be of service—it is constructive rather than destructive.

I assume you don't want your voice to say things you don't mean. I also assume that you don't want your voice to shut off communication between you and others, when this may not be your intention. If so, you can learn to modulate your tone of voice so it accurately reflects your feelings and attitudes. You can do it without voice training. Here's how.

Simply take a few seconds to ask yourself: "What are my objectives in saying what I'm about to say?" Your tone of voice will, in most cases, automatically reflect the objectives you want to accomplish.

Let us say you do something that seems to offend another person. His reactions to you clearly reveal that he is angry, but you don't know why. Your response might be: "I don't know why you're angry." If your objective is to let him know that he had no business reacting the way he did, your voice will convey that attitude. However, if your objective is to find out what you did to incur his wrath, your tone of voice will be more level and convey the feeling that you want to know.

When someone criticizes one of your actions, you might ask yourself: "Do I want to justify my action, make excuses for it, and let him know how disgusted I am with his comment? Or do I want to gracefully accept the criticism, and encourage him to tell me why he reacted the way he did?" Even if you choose to explain your action, you can do so, but not until you let him know that he's entitled to his criticism. Again, you can do it by the tone of voice you use.

Obviously I can't offer examples of how this approach works in every situation. But I can assure you that if you take a few seconds to ask yourself, "What objectives do I want to accomplish with what I'm about to say?" or "What attitudes do I want to convey to this person?" you will substantially increase the accuracy of your communication.

Try it for yourself at home. Take the question, "Would you explain that?" or "What are you doing here?" Experiment by using different inflections, and then ask yourself each time, "What meaning am I conveying?" The meanings are different, aren't they? You can also reverse the process. First determine what attitude you want to transmit, and then ask the questions suggested, or any others that might occur to you. You could also experiment with words like "Hi," or "Yes," or "No."

I recognize there are times when you are so emotionally upset that you are unable to put into practice my suggestion for modulating your tone of voice. And that's okay, too. After all, you're subject to ups and downs like all of us. But I know from experience that if you employ it when you can, it will pay great dividends.

11
Feedback

Many progressive firms actively seek information regarding the purchasing behavior of current as well as potential customers. They also conduct studies to determine employees' attitudes toward management. Using this kind of information, commonly called *feedback*, companies make whatever adjustments and changes are necessary to increase customers' acceptance of their products or services or to improve employees' morale.

Similarly, the feedback entertainers receive from their audiences tells them how well they are coming across. Many performers change their act, even in the middle of their routine, when audience reaction is not favorable.

In the business of living, *the way you respond to another person's words or actions serves as feedback to that individual.* Your responses convey feelings and attitudes which may cause others to either listen to you or turn you off. You can encourage people to be open and honest with you, or to be distrustful of you. You can create a defensiveness in others, or you can stimulate them to engage in a meaningful dialogue with you.

Your feedback can be either useful and constructive or destructive and shut people off. Assuming you want to convey a caring attitude, and assuming you do not want to discourage a healthy give-and-take, let me share five principles of effective feedback. These principles, when put into practice, are certain to improve your skills in relating to others.

103

Describe or Acknowledge—Do Not Judge

If you ever want to place a person on the defensive or make him angry, just tell him what he should or shouldn't feel. I have heard people do this with business associates, as well as with friends and family members. A parent, for example, may tell a youngster who is upset because a friend rejected him: "You shouldn't be sad." Or, a wife, in an effort to placate her husband when he suffers a disappointment at work, may say: "You shouldn't feel disappointed," or "You should feel good that it wasn't worse."

While people who tell others how or what they should or shouldn't feel frequently mean well, such statements usually engender a hostile reaction. A friend of mine who ran for political office was visibly upset when she heard that she lost in a close race. Her husband, who wanted to ease her pain, said: "I don't know why you're upset. You should feel proud you got as many votes as you did." Her response to his innocent, innocuous, and seemingly loving remark was an angry, "Don't tell me how I should feel. I feel lousy."

Why such hostility and anger? The word "should" implies an intellectual judgment, while feelings reflect emotions which are unique to each individual. Feelings are personal; nobody reacts identically to the same situation. What would worry you might be shrugged off as unimportant to someone else. What might upset another person may be inconsequential to you. So how can you say what is a right or wrong feeling for another person?

The fact is that you are not in a position to intellectually judge people's emotions. Others feel and display emotions in their own private way, and as long as they are not directly harming you, you ought to respect those feelings, just as you would want others to respect your unique emotional and pain thresholds. How would you like it if, in response to your scream while he was drilling a tooth, your dentist said, "That shouldn't hurt." His comment would not only be a display of insensitivity, it would not ease your pain.

How, you might ask, do you respond appropriately to other

people's emotions? You can simply acknowledge or describe the emotion: "You seem upset." Or "You look like you've had a hard day." Or "You are understandably disappointed that you didn't get the promotion." Or "You say you hate your job. I suppose there are things about it that cause you to feel that way."

Descriptive and acknowledging feedback tells others that you seem to understand, or at least accept, their emotional state. Such benign comments, which do not deny the other person's emotions, may encourage the individual to elaborate on his or her feelings. Your nonjudgmental reactions would, in all probability, open the door for an interchange of ideas and expression of feelings.

This principle of effective feedback is not applicable when a person expresses his feelings in a destructive way. If someone is angry and shows his feelings by acting violently, you have every right to protect yourself and your property, and to let him know that you think his behavior is "wrong" or "bad."

But even when it comes to judging actions—I'm talking about nonviolent ones—there are effective and ineffective ways of doing it. An example that comes to mind involves a salesman who was padding his expense account. It seems that Bob reported in his monthly expense statement that he had lunch several times, and also took out a particular customer (let's call him John) to dinner on a couple of occasions. When the sales manager saw Bob's expense report he couldn't believe his eyes; John had died two months before. Apparently Bob didn't know about it.

The infuriated sales manager called Bob into his office. After exchanging the usual pleasantries, he asked: "In the last two weeks did you take John out to lunch and dinner *this* many times?" Bob thought for a moment and replied, "Yes, I did." Leaning forward in his chair, the manager blurted out: "You're not only a cheat, but you're a liar too."

The manager had evidence to indict Bob on one infraction, but he felt it necessary to set a trap so he could get him on two counts. Regardless of the fact that Bob was wrong, the manager handled the situation poorly.

This "double whammy" tactic, a common way of dealing

with behavioral problems both at home and in business, is neither honest nor constructive. When you know for certain that a person did something he shouldn't have, don't ask if he did it. Rather, confront him with the fact, and state it as such. *Then* proceed to react in whatever way you feel you must.

Traps are devious; they breed resentment and they don't resolve anything. Honest confrontations are healthier for all concerned. The "did you" type of question is appropriate only when you are not sure whether the other person did what you think he did.

Be Specific

In anger, we frequently say things to others that are not particularly accurate. Words like "never" and "always" crop up in our sentences: "You *never* help around the house" or "You are *always* gone when I need you" or "You *never* listen to me." These generalizations cloud specific truths. More often than not such accusations lack credibility because they are based upon one or several instances of behavior that upset an individual.

Generalizations like "You are a terrible cook" may be a husband's reaction to one poorly prepared meal. Or "You are lazy" may be a parent's admonishment of a youngster who hasn't cleaned his room. A teacher friend of mine told me he was accused of "not being ambitious" when he rejected a promotion to an administrative post.

The problem with these generalizations is that *they disparage the total person rather than the specific action.* Chances are the wife who prepares one or two unsavory meals has cooked at least some tasty meals, and does not merit the "bad cook" label. The youngster who is accused of being "lazy" may very well show initiative in his studies, sports, and other activities. My school-teacher friend was, and still is, actively involved in developing and marketing teaching aids. Of course, he's ambitious, but he is not interested in climbing the academic administrative ladder.

Why do people generalize their attacks? Two reasons: First,

they emphasize their anger by generalizing, and thereby, they believe, strengthen their case. Second, they hope to stimulate the accused to take action by instilling a feeling of guilt. Their reasoning is, "If I make him feel guilty or angry, he will shape up."

Favorable results *can* sometimes be achieved by employing these tactics. I'm sure you've met people who respond to broad accusations with the attitude, "I'll show you how wrong you really are." But, more often than not, people react to generalized attacks with a counterattack. Or they will back off and retreat into their shell without taking the action you desire. Such attacks may scare rather than motivate them.

Criticisms introduced by the phrase "You are" tell the other person that you equate him with the quality you are judging. It's as if you are branding him with a particular characteristic or quality. Understandably, such statements as "You are hostile" or "You are irresponsible" are condemnations that are usually taken personally, creating a defensive posture. After all, the individual as a whole (the "you" part) doesn't feel *all* his acts are hostile or irresponsible.

In leveling criticism at a person, you could be more effective if you took the position that you can disapprove of an individual's behavior without attacking the person's total self. Statements like "Your behavior [be sure to identify it] is offensive to me" are more likely to result in positive change than those beginning with "You are. . . ." To put it differently, you can like an actor but still dislike a specific performance. If that is so, your criticism would be better received if you focused your comments on the performance in question rather than on the actor.

Constructive Criticism

Feedback has two basic functions: (1) *to let others know how we feel about what they say or do;* and (2) *to stimulate changes in their current or future behavior.*

Some behavior can be changed, while other behavior can't. If you want to emotionally disarm someone, just keep hitting that person over the head with what he should have done or said in the past. Keep reminding him of his past mistakes and errors, and continue telling him how stupid he was for saying or doing what he did. This type of feedback is a favorite pastime of people who want to render another individual defenseless.

The pointlessness and destructive effect of such reactions is illustrated in the following dialogue between a husband and wife. They are on their way to a dinner party at his boss's house, and they are running very late. The husband speaks first:

"You're always late." (She does have this tendency.)

"I didn't realize how long a drive it was."

"You should have started dressing earlier."

"I know now. But you should have told me that it was a long drive."

"Yes, but if it weren't for you we wouldn't be rushing like this."

"Okay, it's over with. I can't do anything about it now."

(Later, on their way home, the husband continues.)

"Did you see the look on their faces when we walked in late?"

"Yes, but I told you before that I didn't realize how long it would take us to get there."

"I know, but by coming late we made a bad impression. And it's your fault."

(Several times later, during the course of the week, he reminds her of what she did to him.)

Sound familiar? Similar conversations, with different details, take place frequently between bosses and subordinates, parents and children, husbands and wives, or any other two people who have a close relationship. The specific details don't matter. The question is, Why the badgering? Why, in the above illustration, did the husband continue adding salt to his wife's wound? More important, could the husband have handled the situation differently?

His badgering was a reaction to his own frustration and anger. He felt bad, so he wanted to make her feel bad too. Perhaps if she had expressed her sincere concern and apology early in the conversation he wouldn't have needed to work so hard at making her feel bad.

Could this situation (or others like it) have been handled more constructively? The husband, knowing his wife is frequently late, could have told her in advance how long it would take to get to his boss's house; he could also have told her how important this event was to him. Then, after expressing his initial feelings, and after having made his point, he could have dropped it.

Here are some general principles you can employ when you are irritated by another person's actions.

1. *Make your feelings known.* After all, you are entitled to express how you feel about what the person has done to upset you.

2. *When possible, avoid the use of phrases like "I told you so," "You shouldn't have," or other destructive references to past mistakes.* You can't undo what has happened, so what value is gained by adding insult to injury? Instead, offer positive suggestions about what that person might do the next time a similar situation arises. That is, use the person's errors, mistakes, or inappropriate actions as *tools to teach or guide, rather than as weapons to hurt him.*

If you bring up past mistakes (and if you must introduce them with "You shouldn't have"), follow up your criticisms with specific positive suggestions the person can use as a guide for future actions. Hopefully such feedback will help him to avoid repeating those behaviors which disturb you.

3. When possible, *explain to the person the reasons for your irritation and,* if appropriate, *what benefits would be gained by following your suggestions.* Such explanations may well help that person accept your feelings and point of view. To repeat a statement I made before, you can't expect others to understand your intellectual and psychological makeup. But the more information you offer, the greater your chance of being listened to.

4. Finally, if your irritation is based upon a single and isolated

incident, *don't harp on the mistake after expressing your initial anger.* What's done is done. The person can't retrace his steps, and your anger or unreasonable reactions will not change what has happened. If your criticisms can't serve as an object lesson for guiding a person's future behavior, forget it.

Don't Save Up Your Anger

Some people have a tendency to hold feelings in until one incident incites an eruption and they explode. The incident is like the straw that breaks the camel's back. These people may boil and burn inside, but they do not show their feelings.

Two examples come to mind. The first involves Harry, a twenty-one-year-old college senior, and his father. As the story was told to me, Harry informed his father that he wanted to go to graduate school, but he wasn't sure he could afford it. He asked whether his father could provide financial assistance.

At this point the father let loose with a tirade: "Why should I? You didn't help me cut the grass last summer, and you didn't help me paint the house two summers ago. And three years ago you went on vacation for two weeks when you should have been working. And that's not all. You quit your last job, and were out of work for three weeks. You had no business leaving your job until you had another one!"

The boy was flabbergasted. He had no idea these events over the years were upsetting to his father. Apparently Harry's father had been saving up these feelings for some time.

A variation of the same problem often occurs on the domestic scene. A husband may do things (like coming home late without calling) that infuriate his wife. Rather than expressing her feelings about his behavior at the time, or soon after it happens, she holds it in. She may even make excuses for him: "He can't help it," or "He doesn't mean to be inconsiderate."

After tolerating and being silent about several specific instances of his behavior that have disturbed her, she blows up at one insignificant act. Her reaction is totally out of proportion to the incident that stimulated her attack. Having mustered the courage to speak her mind, she dredges up all her frustrations of the past. Like a prosecuting attorney, she methodically presents all the evidence she has collected to convict him.

Husbands can and often do act the same way as the wife in this story. Furthermore, the problem is not limited to parents and children or husbands and wives. The same type of destructive "sport" goes on between bosses and subordinates as well as between friends or relatives.

It's destructive because it places the other person on the defensive. Chances are the person being attacked doesn't even remember many of the past incidents the attacker cites. Nevertheless, people who use such tactics do it because they believe they need to build a significant case to justify their anger.

You don't need to build a case to justify your feelings. You have a right to feel whatever you feel, and to make your feelings known to the person who has stimulated your reactions. You would be more emotionally honest with yourself and others if you expressed your anger *at an appropriate time,* soon after you became angry. Don't save up your anger. To do so makes mountains out of what may only be molehills. When you express your feelings about an action that offends you, the person knows where he stands. This is an important first step if he wants to modify or explain his behavior.

By saving up your feelings you are violating another principle we discussed earlier—criticizing past behavior the person can't do anything about. Failure to give immediate feedback is like blindfolding a bowler and not telling him which pins he hit. Without this information his effectiveness is substantially diminished. There is nothing to be gained by informing him at the end of the game what he did wrong in each frame.

Don't Impose Feedback

Frequently people will ask your advice on matters of concern to them. When you offer it, they may argue with you. At other times a friend or acquaintance will relate a problem to you, without directly asking for your advice. But because you are a good friend, you feel compelled to tell him what he should or should not do. Again, the friend may argue with you.

More often than not, when you give people advice on personal problems—whether or not it is solicited—you place yourself in a vulnerable position. Do people *really* want your advice, even when they ask for it, or are they actually asking for other viewpoints so they themselves can sort out their feelings? Do they want to be told what to do, or are they really interested in alternative courses of action to consider? Maybe all they want is a sympathetic ear.

You might, if you want to be a good friend, point out the pros and cons of several possible approaches for resolving their dilemmas. *Be careful to present, rather than sell, your ideas.* Then let them make their own decisions.

Suppose, for example, a friend or neighbor asks you, "What should I do about my youngster, who is doing poorly in school?" Your response might be: "You could talk to the teacher, or you could seek professional help." If the person presses and asks you specifically what to do, you might say, "I can't *tell* you what to do, but if I had the problem this is what I would do." Make sure you convey your idea as an opinion rather than as a prescription.

With regard to the individual who merely relates a problem to you, chances are he doesn't want your advice but rather your acknowledgment of the feelings he is experiencing. A safe way of handling such a situation is to be a good listener and to withhold judgments. If you believe you can be of some specific help to the person, you might ask, "Would you like my reactions?" Depending upon how enthusiastically he responds to your offer, you may or may not present your thoughts on the matter.

At this point you might ask, "Do I always have to wait for an invitation to react to another individual's words or actions?" My answer is, "No." If that person's actions are disturbing to you, and cause you discomfort, you obviously can't wait for an invitation to express your feelings. But, when you do, remember the principles discussed earlier.

Summary of Useful Feedback Principles

In general, the purpose of effective feedback is to *make known your feelings and attitudes toward other people's actions and words in ways that are mutually beneficial.* You want the other person to profit from your reactions, but without sacrificing your own honesty or integrity, and without overstepping your bounds. You want to build rather than burn bridges.

To achieve these objectives:

1. Describe or acknowledge other people's feelings, rather than judge them.
2. Criticize specific acts rather than the total individual.
3. Direct your criticisms toward behavior the person can do something about.
4. React to a person's behavior and words as soon as possible. Don't save up your anger.
5. Don't give advice unless you are asked to give it. Even when you are asked, present alternatives the person might consider, rather than specific prescriptions.

12

"Winners" and "Losers"

Popular as they are, the terms "winners" and "losers" are deceptive, because few if any persons can be so simplistically categorized. Nobody I have ever met is consistently either a winner or a loser.

With these reservations in mind, we can still use the terms as convenient labels for two basically different attitudes people employ in their relationships and activities. A "winner's" attitudes are such that he winds up with considerably more successes than failures, while a "loser" fails more than he succeeds because of the peculiar way he views and reacts to his experiences.

These attitudes and the behavior that stems from them influence people's career growth, family relations, and relationships with other people. Before we outline some guidelines for becoming a winner in the business of living, let us look more specifically at the contrasts between these two types of attitudes.

"Losers"

Probably *the single word that best characterizes a loser is "rigidity."* While all of us are creatures of habit and sometimes refuse to bend, losers tend to be *highly* rigid. Rigidity is a way of life that pervades all their activities and relationships. These people have their minds made up; they don't want to be confused by other viewpoints, or even facts. Convinced that they have all the answers, they believe that there is only one way to do things: their way.

All of us approach living with some assumptions. Rigid individuals approach situations and other people with an inflexible set of assumptions and rules for playing each "game"—any interaction or activity—almost as if they were playing by themselves. They are not interested in discovering which rules are appropriate to a given game. They've developed their own formulas for dealing with the world around them, and those are the ones they apply to every situation.

Obviously, since no two "games"—be they a job, a relationship, or a sport—are played by identical rules, their losses are many. Their refusal to develop a "game plan" to fit the situation, or to consider viewpoints other than those similar to theirs, limits their perspective, opportunities, and fund of information for solving problems.

I have, for example, met many university students who doggedly maintain the position that all they want from any course they take is a grade. They know that if they study the material and pay attention in class their objective will be achieved. When I find students like these in courses I teach, I tell them in advance that the principles they will learn are practical. The more they participate in class—ask questions, relate personal examples, and test some of their own ideas—the greater the value they will receive from the course.

Rigid students refuse to budge from their firmly established method of conduct. Because the grade is all-important to them, and they have developed a working formula for obtaining it, they do not change their classroom demeanor. They remain silent, assuming the professor will give them the information they need to do well on the test. Often they do. But they lose out on much of what the course really has to offer.

I've also seen this attitude exhibited by businessmen. Joe is a case in point. During the forties Joe started a small manufacturing firm. It was a struggle, but, being an excellent salesman, he was able to get the business he needed, and to convince those who worked for him to stay with him during those difficult times. His perseverance paid off. His volume of business grew, as did the number of employees and the size of the plant. He was financially successful.

By mid-1960 he had two hundred employees, and his sales volume had jumped substantially. But his profits from 1955 to 1960 remained the same. One of his sons, Harold, a graduate of a reputable business school, analyzed the problem. He informed his father that as he saw it the operation had been run the same way for the past twenty years. He told Joe that if they were to stay in business there would have to be some changes. Up to this point Joe had been doing everything himself, including making all the decisions. Harold suggested that they form departments and hire qualified managers to run them. He also made some other recommendations to increase plant efficiency and profits.

Joe refused to acknowledge the relevance of Harold's analysis. "I've made it on my own this far. I can continue without your help," he told his son. Joe failed to recognize that conditions had changed. The plant was no longer the same size, competition was keener, and Joe was getting older. Although he did not want to accept the idea, the fact was that he could not continue playing this game by the same rules as he had in the past.

As a result of Joe's rigidity, Harold quit one year later, as did several other valuable employees. Sales declined within the next two years, and by late 1960 Joe had declared bankruptcy.

The consequences resulting from Joe's rigidity are minor compared to those that can develop when people in the "helping" professions demonstrate rigidity. I'm referring to people like Art, a grade-school teacher who automatically takes the position that something is wrong with Johnny because he does not respond to Art's teaching methods. Art's explanation is that Johnny probably has a "learning disability" or an "emotional problem." When Johnny's parents propose that the teaching technique might possibly be modified, Art adamantly insists that his methods have been proved to be good.

I'm also talking about the psychologist (or psychiatrist) whose only method for treating patients doesn't work with Ruth. So, instead of assessing the merits of his approach as it applies to Ruth's situation, he tells her she is resisting him and doesn't really want help. He makes *her* the culprit.

The physician who is stymied about a particular problem one of his patients brings to him, but who refuses to refer her to a specialist, is another case in point. "Don't worry about it," or "It'll go away," becomes his standard response when his problem patients suggest that perhaps they ought to consult someone else. It seems these professionals are concerned more with maintaining their image of themselves than with helping their patients.

Such reasoning, whether employed by educators, psychologists, lawyers, or physicians, makes about as much sense as a physician treating a virus with penicillin because it's a miracle drug, even though the patient claims he is allergic to this medicine.

When my wife and I are thoroughly convinced that a professional whose services we employ is rigid, we immediately find a replacement. We cannot afford to deal with people who would sacrifice their clients or patients for their own selfish, nonprofessional interests. It is too dangerous to deal with supposedly responsible people who have all the answers but few if any questions.

Highly rigid people have many qualities in common. They are, to a fault, generally neat, well organized, and compulsively finicky. They also tend to fit people into boxes, almost as if they were dealing with statistics. But while what statistics reveal is very interesting and informative, they conceal what is most vital.

With regard to people, what is most vital is their uniqueness. So, when such people fit someone into a box on the basis of a particular quality or characteristic he exhibits, they are branding the individual. He now is conveniently and safely put into a category of "all people who. . . ." Having appropriately labeled, categorized, and boxed the individual up, they now "know" how to treat him.

Once a rigid person places you in a box, it's almost impossible to get out of it. His tendency is to view you as either an enemy or a friend. As an enemy, everything you say and do is suspect. He will attribute to you negative qualities and characteristics you never knew you had. He will even impute base motives to your well-intentioned actions.

If, for example, he sees you as a selfish person, a gift from you or any generosity you might exhibit would be viewed as phony or as a gesture with strings attached. In short, the only way he could maintain his negative image of you is to interpret your behavior in terms of what he *assumes* to be true. Rather than change his image of you, he would prefer to keep you in the box where you belong.

An attorney friend of mine who worked for a law firm told me about a perfect example of the kind of person I'm talking about. Burt's boss had his set ways of doing things. One day the two of them had a disagreement about the handling of a particular case. My friend lost, of course. From that day on, Burt could do nothing right. Even when he won a couple of difficult cases, his boss shrugged off Burt's success as unimpressive. His response to the first win was, "Anyone could have settled that case," and his reaction to the second settlement was, "That was a routine open-and-shut problem." Burt saw no alternative but to quit.

If you happen to be fortunate enough to be placed in a "friend box" by a rigid person, you can do almost no wrong. He will excuse your errors, undesirable behavior, and anything else you might say or do that would normally be interpreted as unwholesome.

But this kind of rigidity, sometimes called the "halo effect," can also be dangerous. Those who have an angelic view of a person fail to acknowledge his obvious faults and human frailties. The individual who, without question, follows the advice of his physician because he is a "doctor," is a case in point. Or the principal who backs his teacher, regardless of the incriminating evidence against the teacher in a parent-teacher dispute, is another example of "halo" rigidity.

By the way, don't ever try to argue with rigid persons. You can't win. Once they've made up their minds to a particular point of view, it is against their "religion" to be dissuaded. If they feel pessimistic about the way their life is going, they are *certain* it will always be that way; nothing will change, no matter what they do. If you suggested positive steps to improve their lot, or if you gave a "pep talk" in an attempt to alter their views, the response would probably be: "Yes, but you don't understand." In fact, they have "yes, but" answers for just about any new idea you might offer. It's their cordial way of shutting the door on people.

The rigid person's losses become apparent when he takes an all-or-nothing stance in his business dealings and his relations with people. His attitude is, "If I can't have it completely my way, I don't want anything." As a result he frequently winds up with nothing or substantially less than he could have had.

I'm not sure whether it's false pride, lack of trust in their judgments, or a real inability to see things and people in any but a black-and-white way. But the fact is that the real world is in "living color" and also contains shades of grays, so when a person views a three-dimensional spectacular with tunnel vision, his losses have to exceed his gains.

That is why the rigid person is a "loser." He misses out on others' genuine and well-meaning concerns, and ignores many experiences that could be beneficial to him. Instead, he holds on to beliefs that do not serve his best interests. In short, he insists on reducing to simple formulas those complex problems that require intelligent judgments and evaluations.

"Winners"

About eight months ago I was to give a four-hour presentation on "Achieving Your Potential" to a group of criminal investigators. Mine was to be the only nontechnical subject presented during this week-long in-service training program. Having given talks of this nature many times, I knew that this group would be interested; all I had to do was present the material just as I had in the past.

After talking for ten or fifteen minutes I got the distinct feeling they weren't with me. There is nothing more uninspiring to a speaker than looking out at an audience that appears to be hypnotized. To break things up a bit, I asked, "Are there any comments or questions?" One person sheepishly raised his hand, which I acknowledged. His question dealt with a topic I was planning to delve into later in my talk. But I sensed that it probably reflected a personal problem. I answered his question in depth.

More hands went up; I handled their questions and comments the same way. As long as there were questions and problems they wished to discuss, I said, I would set aside my prepared notes and address myself to *their* concerns. Their applause showed that they approved.

The audience came alive. More important, I was able to cover more material than I had originally planned and in a way that was meaningful to this particular group. By using the audience, instead of my outline, as my guide, what could have been a disastrous morning turned into a productive one. For me, this experience also reinforced the value of being flexible, of rolling with the punches.

The flexible person has three basic qualities which distinguish him from the rigid individual.

1. He is discriminating.

2. He asks questions.

3. He is reasonably secure with himself, both emotionally and intellectually.

While flexible people may sometimes prejudge a person or the outcome of an event, their powers of discrimination eventually win out. They evaluate a person's behavior on its own merits. If, for example, a mediocre employee does a commendable job on a particular project, a flexible manager will compliment the specific performance. Admittedly, such a manager may not like this person, but he will not permit his attitude to influence his evaluation of specific meritorious actions.

Flexible people tend to pick beneficial qualities and behavior in others, and temporarily disregard those which may be distasteful. They will not, as do rigid people, discard a whole bushel of apples even though several may be rotten. Similarly, they would not assume, if a person exercises poor judgment under one set of conditions, that this individual should *never* be trusted again. Recognizing the danger of generalizing, they assess the meaning of *each* action and react accordingly. They realize that most people are not as predictable as rigid people would like to think.

The flexible person also evaluates situations. When he enters a "game," he first looks around to see what it's all about. He looks for opportunities; he tries to assess what emotional, intellectual, or financial benefits he can gain from his involvement. He can't afford to jump in head first, or turn his back on a situation, if he doesn't know anything about it.

He also tries to determine in what ways the situation he is evaluating relates to similar "games" he has played. If there are similarities, he has experiences he can draw upon. Of course, he also determines what differences there might be so he can make appropriate adjustments.

Having made his evaluation, he is then able to determine whether he wants to play this "game." Assuming he does, he plays by the established rules. Otherwise, he finds himself another "game," if that is possible.

Going back to the example I used earlier, my flexible students wait to see how I conduct myself in class, and what the subject is all about. Once they realize that it isn't the run-of-the-mill course, they test me with a question or two. When I show my concern and interest in them, their class involvement is what I hope for. And, naturally, they get more than a grade from the course. *That's* a winner—a person who signs up for a class and receives course credit, a grade, *plus* therapy.

The ability to ask questions is another valuable tool of the flexible person. Recognizing that he is not an expert on everything and everyone, he knows that the only way he can learn is to ask. But his inquiries have a purpose beyond merely acquiring knowledge. The more information he can gather, the better equipped he is to make well-thought-out and logical decisions. Since the kinds of judgments a flexible person makes are more complex (because his world consists of grays), he needs all the input available. Being more interested in results and in achieving his objectives than in protecting his image or favorite techniques, he opts for the *best* way, which may not necessarily be *his* way.

Flexible managers I have known admit when they've been wrong. They are willing to scrap their ideas for better ones that subordinates present. Naturally, they will investigate the merits, as well as the negative features, of the ideas and opinions presented. They will then study them, constantly keeping in mind what they want to accomplish, and then make their decisions. For them formulas and favored approaches are useful tools, but when they no longer serve a meaningful purpose, they are discarded. "Sacred cows" do not have a significant place in a flexible person's mode of thinking; they would only contaminate his judgment.

To be flexible one has to be reasonably sure of himself, both emotionally and intellectually. Such a person is saying, in effect, "I can bend, roll with the punches, or change directions in midstream because I feel confident that I will not lose my balance." The flexible person maintains his balance because he is willing to learn and to make whatever adjustments are necessary to achieve the results he is seeking.

He also gains respect from the people he deals with and takes the best from what they have to offer. He relies on his fund of inner resources to help him make judgments about specific problems and people. Because he is adaptable and can cope with change, he is a winner in a constantly changing environment.

Guidelines for Becoming a Winner

Relatively few people are winners in everything they undertake. Some may be winners in business, but not at home; others are winners with friends, but not in their careers. And so it goes. But with the help of three basic principles, we can all try:

1. *Be flexible. Evaluate* people's behavior rather than putting them into boxes. The world consists mostly of grays, rather than of pure blacks and whites.
2. *Be flexible. Listen* to what others have to say. You don't have all the answers, nor do they. Perhaps you can learn from each other.
3. *Be flexible.* If a particular approach, method, or technique isn't working, *consider using another one.* Remember, you are interested in results.

13

How to Disagree Constructively

No progressive company can operate effectively unless it maintains a balanced set of books. As people in the business of living, we also have to maintain internal consistency—an inner balance which enables us to be in harmony with ourselves. Since we are so complex, this is often a difficult objective, for the "books" we have to balance are not mere numbers posted on a ledger sheet.

Our complicated filtering devices have to juggle whatever values, attitudes, and knowledge we have learned in the past, and relate them to the daily input of the business of living. We also have emotional experiences which must be balanced against other feelings we have experienced in the past. The process our human accounting system has to go through to sift out the relevant from the irrelevant, deceptions from truth, and honest from dishonest input, would boggle the most sophisticated computer.

Why People Disagree

Our values and attitudes provide us with a foundation for maintaining intellectual and emotional equilibrium. *Values are strongly held beliefs,* deeply ingrained in each individual, that are frequently expressed as judgments of what is "good" or "bad,"

124

"right" or "wrong." Values also influence our evaluations of and attitudes toward people and objects.

We begin to develop these values, or beliefs, early in life, and continue to build on them as long as we live. We have values about religion, politics, people, and anything else that affects us personally. Having this foundation, we can go about our business of living, which is to do and say those things that reflect our values and attitudes.

Regardless of how strong your beliefs are, *you need to feel you are not alone in your thinking.* To validate or to confirm your values you, like all of us, seek support from others (perhaps this is one reason why so many decisions in commercial businesses are made by committees). The greater the number of people you can get to agree with you, the more secure you feel about your beliefs. This is particularly true if your endorsements come from sources which are important to you—your family, friends, boss, or business acquaintances.

Validation by consensus is a common method for gaining emotional support for what we believe in. This is why it is so important to convince others that our decisions are correct. It is as if we are saying, "I'm fairly certain of my beliefs, but if I can get others to agree with me, I can be more confident." In fact, attempting to convince others of our point of view, as opposed to simply informing them, is one of our main conversational objectives.

Your need to be liked or to be popular is another sign of the very human need for validation from others. Their approval seems to increase the value you place on yourself as a person. Such recognition tells you that, regardless of what you might think of yourself, you are accepted by others.

The amount of approval or endorsement we seek varies from person to person; some need more than others. From my observation, the more ambitious a person is, the greater his need for winning *many* people over to his side. Ambitious people rarely receive all the plaudits they feel they deserve, or their appetites require.

Obviously, you can't expect to gain support for every belief you stand for or every opinion you express. After all, others, like you, need to keep their own strong beliefs and unique "accounting systems" in balance. When you advance a point of view inconsistent with another person's values, you create a disharmony, or "dissonance," within that person. Unable to tolerate this discomfort, he's got to protect himself, just as you would if you felt your foundation was being threatened. Before we discuss possible ways of handling such inner disharmony, as well as effective methods of disagreeing, let us take a closer look at why and how this dissonance occurs.

What Is Dissonance?

If you are to maintain emotional and intellectual balance, you cannot embrace two values that are mutually exclusive. Nor can you, at the same time, accept two opposing attitudes or facts.

You cannot, for example, believe that it is now both night and day. Nor can you be both a staunch Republican and a dedicated Democrat. You cannot believe in running an honest business, while cheating your clients. These inconsistencies—or "dissonances"—would create conflicts that would, to use the vernacular, "blow your mind."

Now, let's look at a few practical examples of the kinds of dissonance people encounter. Do you recall Jim, whom I mentioned in the first chapter? The dissonance he was facing was this: his major belief was that by building a financially successful manufacturing firm he would be happy, but his career success actually resulted in personal misery. *His feelings were inconsistent with his beliefs, hence the dissonance.*

Mark's situation is also one many people can identify with. He was brought up to believe that if he worked hard, kept his mouth shut, and did not make waves, he would be rewarded for his efforts. Mark has been dedicated and loyal to one company for twenty years. He rose to foreman, a position he has held for fifteen years, but since then has been passed over many times for promotion. When one of the newer and younger employees was promoted to a position Mark wanted, he finally questioned his superior. "You're conscientious and you're a good worker," Mark's boss told him, "but you're too quiet, you show no initiative. This company needs aggressive people with ideas." Apparently the qualities that actually got recognition were in direct conflict with Mark's beliefs. He was thrown so completely off balance that he went into a severe depression.

Dissonance is also created within a person who has a favorable self-concept, but who is mistreated by friends or business associates. The conflict, as viewed by the person, may be stated in the form of a question: "If I am such a good, reasonable, and likable person, why am I being treated so shabbily?" The same type of reasoning holds true of an individual who does not believe himself worthy of human kindness, but is nevertheless treated with respect and dignity. His question becomes, "If I'm not deserving of this treatment, why am I getting it?"

In short, *dissonance problems are those that raise questions or doubts about our beliefs, perceptions, attitudes, and feelings.* When our thoughts and feelings, which we generally consider to be "right" and "good" for us, are challenged, we experience discomfort—a psychological imbalance. Since we cannot tolerate this condition very long, we look for ways to achieve inner harmony.

Ways of Resolving Dissonance

Faced with two conflicting views about a particular issue, a person can exercise one of three options for resolving the dissonance. I will explain these options by relating them to a specific problem.

Problem: Mary is a twenty-four-year-old journalist who has a degree with honors from a reputable college; she also has three years' experience with a small suburban newspaper. She left her job to accept a better-paying position as a copywriter with an advertising agency. Envisioning herself as a bright, independent, and creative writer, she felt her talents would be recognized quickly.

After six months on the job Mary was still involved in nothing more than routine and mundane work. The fact that she had not yet received more challenging assignments did not square with her image of herself.

Options: 1. Mary could take the position that her boss must be absolutely blind. How could he not recognize her talents? He must be wrong in his evaluation, and doesn't know what he's doing. She might also reason that he must be anti-women, and believes in keeping them in their place. Such negative assumptions about her boss, even if not expressed orally, will be reflected in her future performance. But by attacking him, Mary is able to hold on to her image that she is a highly capable, creative person.

(By the way, it is natural to take offense at anyone who fails to endorse our beliefs, and one's initial reaction is to attack with "You're wrong." When you attack in this way you are implying, "If you don't buy what I'm selling [ideas, abilities, or opinions], you are not a friend. You might even be an enemy whom I must protect myself against." But isn't it possible that what you're "selling" is inappropriate to the other person's needs, or that he is unable to use your ideas or services? Just because you consider something "right" or "good" from your perspective doesn't mean it is right for others.)

2. Mary's second option is to adopt the attitude that perhaps she's not as good as she thought she was. After all, being a top student and working for a small newspaper are meager credentials for the big world of business. She might conclude that she ought to consider herself fortunate to have this job, and that she would do well to lower her aspirations.

Some women—and men—would wince at this type of reasoning. But when you adjust your aspiration level so that it is consistent with and within the range of your speed of growth, you maintain inner harmony. I'm not necessarily recommending this self-deprecating route as a way of resolving dissonance, but it is one approach.

3. The "I'm wrong, you're right" as well as the "You're wrong, I'm right" approaches for restoring inner balance are extremes. And, as is true of many extremes, they have only limited applicability. But there is a third direction Mary could take which to me seems more reasonable. She and her boss might *both* be right.

Her reasoning would be as follows: "I'm good—I've proved that—but perhaps there are factors I hadn't considered which are holding me back in this job." Taking this position, her next step would be to obtain additional information which would help her evaluate her dissonance. She might confront her boss and ask him outright why she hasn't received more challenging work, and how long it will take before she does. Or she might ask him what he thinks of her ability as a copywriter, or might she be better off returning to newspaper writing? Without this information she is not able to resolve the problem that is plaguing her.

Let me tell you what Mary actually did. She considered all three options, but finally decided on the last one. Her boss assured her that her abilities were quite good, but that she needed some specific experience which she did not previously have. With this information she tempered her negative thinking and proceeded to sharpen her skills. Within three months after their talk she was given her first major creative project; her growth has been steady and as of this writing she is still with the firm she started with.

In the first two approaches, you make assumptions that are not necessarily correct. The attitudes and actions that flow from these assumptions may prove self-defeating. In the third approach you take the position that you have insufficient data to make a logical decision. *Resolving dissonance is like solving any problem; the more information you have available, the fewer guesses you will need to make.*

Mary was fortunate. She had a boss who was understanding and sensitive, and she did not need to argue with him about anything he said. They were able to reach an understanding so that she did not have to alter her basic beliefs in herself and her abilities, and he did not need to give her challenging assignments before he felt she was ready.

Alternatives to "You Are Wrong"

If you are like many people, your first reaction, when someone advances a point of view that doesn't coincide with yours, is to say "You're wrong" or "You're crazy." Such comments generally get people's backs up and result in a "No I'm not–Yes you are" type of dialogue. On occasion these offensive-defensive arguments even stoop to name-calling.

If you disagree with the other person, chances are you have some objective evidence that seems to contradict the idea presented. Or, you may have had a personal experience that this person's idea or value does not account for. Under these conditions, you could suggest your disagreement in the form of a question: "Assuming what you are saying is true, how would you explain [relate your experience or contradictory evidence]?" What you are in effect doing is asking him to resolve your dissonance. Now the discomfort is on his shoulders. Such a question also gives the person an opportunity to modify his original position without losing face, as is illustrated in the following examples.

Recently, while we were discussing the subject of motivation, one of my students stated that "to be really successful you have to have pull. Without it you don't have a chance." By "pull" he meant knowing the "right" people, and coming from an influential family.

"If that is so," I said, "how do you explain the financial success of people like Ray Kroc of McDonald's, Colonel Sanders of Kentucky Fried Chicken, and W. Clement Stone?" I didn't think it was necessary to cite more than a few examples.

"Well, that's true," he conceded. "But pull does help if you have it." "It never hurt anyone," I replied. I don't believe our conversation would have been as productive or amiable had I degraded his initial statement.

If the other person flatly rejects the evidence or experiences you present, he sounds like a person who has his mind made up. Since you can't change the thinking of people like that, you can confidently discontinue your discussion.

Not all disagreements are based upon differences in values and attitudes. Some are a result of differing individual preferences. Under these conditions, rather than knocking the other person, simply state your position and your reasons for your preference. If you feel confident about your point of view, stick with it. Remember, everyone is entitled to his opinion. But telling another person that his opinion is "wrong," just because it doesn't agree with yours, doesn't make sense either. His opinion may be right for him. This you can acknowledge without sacrificing your integrity or creating dissonance for yourself.

Sometimes, in order to establish the "rightness" of their own position, or to try to control you, people bait you so that you will argue with them. At parties, for example, when the word gets out that I'm a psychologist, someone will approach me and unload his anger toward "shrinks." Assuming he's had one or two unfortunate experiences, my typical comment is, "I suppose you've run into some bad ones?" Then he tells me about the one he had trouble with, and those whose scars are still not healed conclude their monologue, "I wouldn't trust any of them."

Instead of falling into the trap of defending "shrinks," or discussing their concerns rationally—not a reasonable course of action—I have learned that a simple acknowledgment of their concern, and a simple statement of how I feel, works well. I say, "I'm sorry about your experience, but I would like to think not all shrinks are bad. A few may even be good." Then I excuse myself.

At times you may disagree with a person on purely emotional grounds, with no hard evidence to negate what the other person said. You *feel* you must disagree. My suggestion here is, again, to acknowledge the person's right to his belief, and then state your ideas if you wish. You might even admit to the fact that you can't offer any reasonable explanations for your nonagreement—it's just a gut reaction.

Another rule I have found useful in handling disagreements is the "spoonful of sugar principle." As anyone who has seen *Mary Poppins* knows, a spoonful of sugar helps the medicine go down. And so it is with reactions you might have toward what someone says.

If you can, introduce your disagreements with a positive statement about the other person and his position. You might say, "There are merits to what you say; however, [introduce your point of disagreement]." *Your compliment or acknowledgment of the individual's idea increases his tolerance for whatever "medicine" you have to dish out.* To rephrase a principle we've already discussed, you are in disagreement with something a person has said or done, rather than with the individual.

My final recommendation for constructively handling disagreements works effectively when criticism is leveled against you, or when someone asks you to do something dissonant with your understanding of what you should be doing. Rather than attacking the other person, take the position that perhaps *your* perceptions are not clear. Comments like "I didn't quite understand what you meant" or "I apparently wasn't aware of my obligations. Could you explain them to me?" or "I am confused about what the priorities are. Can you help me sort them out?" are preferable to a "You didn't. . . ." reaction.

When you accept the burden for what may be another person's shortcomings, you are more likely to get what you want—an explanation or other information. The more information you have, the better prepared you will be to evaluate the criticism or request. You're not going to get very far if you react to hurt feelings by striking back.

While I've discussed some alternatives to dealing with disagreements without being disagreeable, resolving differences and conflicts is not always possible. Some people may disagree simply because they want to irritate you. Others are so rigid that they can't possibly change. If you encounter either of those situations, don't bother. Your business is too valuable to waste your time on situations like that.

On the other hand, you may learn a great deal from honest disagreement, if it is matched with open exchange. *Listening* may provide you with the information you need to understand why there is a disagreement, as well as clues about how to resolve it. You may discover that your ability to respect another person's point of view, even when you don't share it, is in and of itself one of the most effective means of persuasion.

And who knows, what you learn from honest disagreement may lead you to the kind of healthy compromise that does more than anything to help your business flourish.

Part 4

MANAGING
YOUR EMOTIONS

14

Feelings Can Be Assets

During your business day you are subject to many emotional reactions, some of which you keep inside, some of which you express. Frequently these feelings crop up without warning: you may be sitting alone in the privacy of your home when a pleasant or unpleasant thought suddenly occurs to you. Or you may be with other people when a comment someone makes triggers off an emotional reaction.

Emotions require expression. "Listen to me and do something about these feelings," they tell you. "Don't just ignore them."

If you hear yourself saying, "But how do I know if I have a right to feel this way? I'm not sure how I should respond," you're not alone. Frankly, this is a common reaction to feelings. Other typical responses are "I don't know what I feel" and "What should I be feeling?"

Many individuals seem to be afraid to face up to their emotions. They are also not altogether certain that if they expressed their feelings their means of expression would be acceptable to others. For these people the image they create—what other people will think of them—becomes more important than their own emotional health. More responsive to the "ghosts" of their parents, who told them what they "should" or "should not" feel, they have difficulty listening to their own inner voices and good judgment.

Recently, when I took my family out to dinner, I overheard two conversations at the table adjoining ours. At one table an excited youngster was saying rather loudly, "Boy, this is good!" The mother responded quickly, "Shhh, keep quiet and eat." At the other table a little girl was crying because her balloon had burst. Her father, apparently embarrassed by his daughter's behavior, said, "If you don't stop crying you'll have to wait in the car until we're finished."

One of my patients came to me because his wife could not tolerate his blandness. Nothing would excite or upset him. If he didn't breathe or move, she said, no one would know he was alive. But an active ulcer and high blood pressure—his badges of "courage" for containing his emotions—reminded him that he was very much alive.

During one of our sessions he related an incident that occurred when he was twelve years old. "I remember how excited I was about getting the lead in a school play," he told me. "I ran home, anxious to relate the good news to my mother. I'll never forget her comment. She said, 'Okay, go out and play.' When my father came home that night I got up enough enthusiasm to share my great accomplishment with him. All he said was, 'That's nice.'"

There were other exciting moments in his youth that had not been enthusiastically received by his parents. "I wasn't even allowed to get upset," he said. "Once in my freshman year in high school there was a party to which a number of my friends were invited, but not me. I felt left out. It was Friday night and there I was all alone feeling sorry for myself. When my father came into the kitchen and saw me crying, he said, 'Quit acting like a baby.' He didn't even ask why I was crying." As I discovered in future sessions, there were a number of such incidents where he could express neither joy nor sadness without being ridiculed or ignored. After a while he learned to hold his feelings in.

As these stories illustrate, many people are taught at an early age not to express their emotions. Is it any wonder that by the time they become adults these individuals consider it safer to keep their feelings to themselves? While they may think it more appropriate or more sophisticated, in the long run it is not healthy to completely stifle emotions. Perhaps this is why sensitivity-training programs have become so popular. Through retraining, many people may learn to trust their feelings and to express these emotions constructively.

In the business of living, emotions take at least two forms. One is the inner feelings you experience. These represent *private* ways of inwardly reacting to your thoughts and experiences. These feelings are neither right nor wrong; they just are. Nobody can fault you for feeling a particular way, whether you are feeling good or bad, happy or sad, sick or healthy.

But emotions also need to be *expressed*. If held in or ignored for too long, they create battles inside you. It's their way of gaining your attention. When you fail to respond, they continue to haunt you or they may find some physical target; usually it's in the gut. Sometimes they can paralyze you to the point that you become unable to see things clearly. Even positive emotions, like joy or enthusiasm, can go sour if you do not respect their right to free expression.

When you allow your emotions to be expressed, their release serves as a safety valve. By being emotionally expressive you can be yourself; you don't need to hide behind a mask. You can feel truly alive when you vocalize your feelings to yourself (or to those you trust) and accept them as an integral part of you. Only when you hear yourself saying what you feel can you begin to sort out the confusion inside you.

Emotions, like time and money, can work to your benefit or they can be misdirected and dissipated; it all depends on how you use them. There are both healthy and unhealthy ways of expressing your feelings. *Knowing how to respond to your inner voices is the key to emotional health.* Expressing your feelings honestly, while maintaining your standards of good judgment, is therapeutic. To laugh heartily when you feel like it, to cry when you are sad, to compliment others when you feel it is warranted, or to express anger when you are upset and disappointed—these are perfectly legitimate and natural human expressions; don't deprive yourself of them.

In responding to your inner voices, the first step is to *identify the nature of your feelings.* Once you have done that you can make some judgments about how to deal appropriately with them. While there is no one clear-cut way to handle each specific emotion, I would like to offer some methods which have worked for me and many people I've seen professionally.

Because most people find it more difficult to handle so-called negative emotions, like guilt, worry, and anger, let's deal with them first. Later in this chapter, we'll discuss expressing so-called positive emotions.

Guilt. Guilt is the feeling a person gets from passing judgment on himself for things he should have said or done but didn't, or about things he did say or do but shouldn't have. Implied in his judgment is the notion that his actions, reactions, or failure to act contradict what he believes is "right."

Who determines what is right? In the final analysis the individual does, on the basis of what he has learned and experienced during his years of living. Therefore, what produces guilt feelings in one person will not faze another.

Feelings of guilt, if not resolved, can be and frequently are destructive. They will eat away at you, drain you, and cause you unnecessary anguish. On the other hand, many feelings of guilt can be dealt with on a conscious level. When this happens, these feelings can be positive forces—if your discomfort leads you to take constructive steps toward overcoming your feelings.* Let me illustrate with an example:

Sam is a twenty-seven-year-old accountant whose ambition is to become a partner with the firm where he is employed. "I can't relax," he told me at our first meeting. "I feel guilty doing it.

---

* There are also guilt feelings people carry around with them from childhood. These are deeply buried and require professional help to resolve. It is beyond the scope of this book to deal with such problems.

When I get uptight I take some medication, which helps to unwind me. But I don't want to take pills all my life."

"What might relax you?" I asked.

"Sometimes I would just like to sit and do nothing, or maybe read a book for fun. But every time I try that I become even more uptight. I feel guilt because I think of all the things I should be doing. So I pick myself up and find something to do around the house."

I asked, "Who told you you should be working all the time?"

"No one," he replied, "but I feel like I'm wasting my time unless I'm doing something constructive. And relaxing is wasting time. Yet I would like to be able to do that without feeling guilty about it."

Sam's problem brings back memories of my early school years. One day I was looking out the window, thinking great thoughts. Upset by what she saw, the teacher yelled at me, "Look busy!" When I turned back to my desk and began to doodle, this seemed to satisfy her. While I was being less productive than before, at least I *looked* busy.

Probably many people can relate to this experience; it's part of the so-called work ethic. Somewhere along the way most of us have been taught to believe that observable action is synonymous with productivity. Since thinking cannot be observed, it is considered nonactivity. I suspect that Sam's guilt had its roots in this type of illogical reasoning. I offered him another way of viewing his conflict about relaxing.

I explained to Sam that relaxation is productive. He is doing something, even though he is not working; he is recharging his batteries. Resting, reading, or taking a walk prepare him for the next day's work activity. "Think of it as an investment in yourself," I told him. My strategy was to have him make a *positive* judgment about his desire to relax.

Sam never thought of relaxation as a productive process. But he decided to give it a try. He started out by taking his full lunch breaks outside the office, rather than eating at his desk or grabbing a bite on the run. Later, after he was fully convinced that he "should" relax, Sam took fifteen-minute breaks in the morning and afternoon. He would just sit quietly with his eyes closed and think about nothing. He no longer felt guilty about relaxing, particularly when he realized the tonic effect it had on him.

The kinds of guilt feelings illustrated in this example arise out of conflicts. In effect, the person condemns himself for choosing one compelling course of action over another equally irresistible one. The executive who feels guilty about working late at night because he thinks he should be with his family, or the mother who feels guilty about spending a day with her friends rather than doing chores around the house, are other examples of this problem.

When such situations arise, rather than harboring the guilt, ask yourself: "Is there a legitimate reason for making the choice I did?" In short, *to relieve your guilt you have to convince yourself that your choice is a good one*. If you can't in good conscience do that, you have no other alternative, short of living with the agony, than to go with the other option. In the case of Sam, if he were not able to sell himself on the virtue of relaxing, he would have to continue working himself to death.

Another form of guilt is exemplified by those people who condemn themselves for past deeds or misdeeds. I can almost hear them saying, "I shouldn't have done this or that," or "I could have done this instead of that." Having committed what they consider to be an unpardonable act, they punish themselves relentlessly. Their regrets fester until they are convinced that they have paid a handsome price for their actions.

An advertising executive related to me how guilty she felt when she impulsively fired one of her junior copywriters. "I shouldn't have done it," she said. "For the past two weeks I've been thinking about what I did, and how wrong I was for firing her. How stupid of me."

Okay, so she made a bad decision. But under the circumstances, and at that particular moment, she did what she thought was right. Does feeling guilty change what happened? Obviously not.

I recall hearing a well-known actor talk about how he learned this lesson while still a student in acting school. After he finished giving a performance, the director complimented him on his efforts. The actor responded, "I could have done better." The director replied sternly, "I don't ever want to hear you say that again. Any time you give a performance, it is the best you can do at that moment. That doesn't mean that an hour from now it won't be better or that yesterday you might not have done a better job. But when you do anything, assuming you are conscientious, you are doing your best at that time."

This principle applies to everything we do. We must believe that, *given the conditions—our frame of mind, the barometric pressure, and the position of the moon—the particular action we have taken was all we could have done.*

So what do we do about the guilt associated with our past actions? There are, as far as I'm concerned, three possible courses of action to relieve this feeling. First, you can *apologize to the person you have hurt.* Second, *forgive yourself.* After all, you're only human and you are entitled to make mistakes. At the same time, try not to repeat your errors. Third, *when possible, rectify the error.* In the case of the advertising executive, I suggested that she try to rehire her employee.

Worry. In essence, *worry is a fear of anticipated future events.* It stems from a person's deep concern about whether he will be able to handle problems or experiences he believes will arise. People worry about being able to pay their bills, the security of their jobs, meeting deadlines, fulfilling social responsibilities, and a myriad of other future uncertainties. What they are afraid of is some unpleasant outcome—a loss, an embarrassment, an unfavorable reaction from others, or being wrong.

Like guilt, mild worry can be a moving force—a preparation for constructive action. But, if the person is preoccupied with his fear, it can be emotionally taxing and even paralyzing. Chronic worriers fret about things they have absolutely no control over, as well as about things they can influence but refuse to.

Whether or not worry serves a constructive purpose depends on what you do with it. In dealing with this feeling you can begin by asking yourself: "What specifically am I concerned about? What am I afraid will happen?" After you have identified the source of your feeling, you might then ask yourself: "Is there a legitimate reason for my concern?" I have known many people who, after questioning the legitimacy of their worry, decided that there was really nothing to be concerned about.

One example that comes to mind involves Olga, who was planning a large dinner party for her husband's professional friends as a public-relations gesture. Since she had never planned anything like this before, she was terrified at the prospect. By the time she related her worry to me, she had already sent out invitations and made the catering and all other proper arrangements. "So what are you worried about?" I asked.

"I guess I'm worried that the guests won't have a good time," she replied. "I'm worried that it won't come off as well as I would like it to."

I then questioned her about her preparations, thinking that perhaps she didn't know how to go about planning such an event. "How sure are you that you've done all you could to prepare for the party?"

"I've done everything possible. The catering service came highly recommended, the children are sleeping at their friends' house, and we've got plenty of room."

"Then you've done everything possible to ensure that the party runs smoothly," I said.

"I guess I have," she responded. "The rest is up to the guests themselves. If they come to have a good time, they will. Why shouldn't they?" (By the way, the party was a success.)

Suppose, however, there is a legitimate reason for being worried. Your next step is to ask yourself: "What am I going to do about it? What courses of action are available to me in preventing or solving this potential problem?" Or, to put the question differently, "What can I do to rid myself of this troubled feeling?"

You know for a fact that worrying alone accomplishes nothing more than to make you miserable. So the only logical approach is to *do all you can to prepare yourself for the problem you anticipate, or to take whatever actions you believe are appropriate to diminish your agony.* One thing is certain: As long as you occupy your valuable time with brooding about what might happen, you drain yourself of the energy you could be using more productively.

There are times, of course, when no course of action is available, and you are still concerned about the possible negative outcome of an event. Take the case of a person whose worry is that he will not get the promotion he is hoping for. This individual must tell himself, assuming he has done all he could to place himself in a favorable light, that burdening himself with this feeling will not accomplish his objective. He would help himself if he diverted his energies by working, playing, or even thinking about what he would do in the event that the promotion didn't come through.

The point is that unless your worries, which frequently take the form of "What would happen if . . . ?" lead to planning of alternative courses of action, they are wasteful. Work at shaking the thought and do things that will get your mind off the worry —at least for the time being.

Anger. We become angry when our sense of rightness is threatened or violated, our image of ourself is in jeopardy, our expectations or desires are not fulfilled, or, to be more general, when we perceive a current or impending obstacle to an objective.

As is true of guilt and worry, anger is a common human emotion. Like the other two emotions, anger needs to be expressed. Stifling it until it hurts you inside is deadly, as any good physician will tell you. The person who feels it's important to maintain peace at any cost may wind up paying with his physical health. When the voice inside you says, "I'm hurting and the hurt makes me mad," you would do well to listen and respond.

The question is, *How do you express your anger,* and under

what conditions is it appropriate? The question implies that you have to make some judgments about how, when, and to whom you express your anger.

There are, of course, times when you seem to have no control over your feelings. In this case, blowing up may be the most natural thing to do. Occasionally that's all right, if it makes you feel better. But many times, when you do have a choice, giving in to your natural impulses is *not* the most appropriate way of expressing this emotion.

To maintain a profitable business, everything we do should contribute to the growth, development, and maintenance of this enterprise. With this objective in mind, when someone or something makes you angry you would do well to ask yourself, "*If I express it, what good will it do me?*" It only takes a second, and it puts the thing about which you are angry in perspective. I'm not saying that you shouldn't acknowledge your feeling. To do so is therapeutic. You might say to yourself, or to whoever will listen, "Boy, that makes me mad." Then forget it. But don't let the feeling get out of control or stew about it. There are some things over which it simply doesn't pay to waste your energy by losing your temper.

Recently I was in a department store and was unable to find what I wanted. There wasn't a salesperson to be found, and that made me mad. So I approached the woman at the cash register and asked her, "Aren't there any salespeople in this department?" To which she replied, "I'm working as fast as I can." Of course, I wasn't judging *her*, but that's the way she took it. As I felt myself becoming increasingly upset, I asked myself, "What will I gain by getting angry at her or anyone else?" When the answer came back, "Nothing," I decided to simply wait until she was available to help me.

Another, related, question you might ask yourself is, "*How will my expressing anger alter the situation?*" Or, to put the question differently, "Does it really matter to the person in question whether or not I'm mad?" In many instances the anger you express falls on deaf ears, so why bother? There are many people and things in life you can't change. Once you recognize that fact, you will save your emotional energy for more constructive activities.

By taking a moment to think, you are giving yourself the luxury of reflecting about the thing that's disturbing you. If, in your judgment, your anger can serve a constructive purpose, by all means express it and then take steps to resolve the problem that's causing the feeling. Make sure, of course, that you choose a suitable place and time. Reprimanding someone in the presence of others, or when the other person is preoccupied with something else, does nothing more than embarrass you and the individual with whom you are angry.

In summary, you have every right in the world to get angry. You also have a right to express this emotion. But before you do, *think about how your expression of this emotion can serve your interests without necessarily destroying others.* (You might review the chapter on *feedback* to remind you of more specific methods of doing this.)

Expressing Pleasant Emotions

Enthusiasm, laughter, and other expressions of pleasant emotions are uplifting and even infectious. When you feel happy and excited inside, and your inner voices say, "You're having fun. You're enjoying yourself," do you respond? Or do you play it cool and avoid allowing yourself to let go and express your true feelings?

There are at least three reasons why you may have difficulty expressing positive emotions. First, you may have learned that mature people are supposed to take happy events in stride; if you express your excitement about a joyful experience, you may be put down by others for "acting like a kid." By playing it cool, you protect yourself against such criticism. At the same time, though, you are depriving yourself of the good feelings that come from such expressions.

Another possible reason for containing your enthusiasm is

that you may be afraid that you are setting yourself up for a severe "downer"; whatever you're excited about may not last. Or, if you anticipate a positive event, you may consider it safer to keep the lid on your enthusiasm in case the event doesn't occur. By holding back your expression of positive feelings, you are minimizing the extent of your possible disappointment.

If you do that, aren't you cheating yourself? That kind of reasoning is like wearing a raincoat while the sun is shining, just in case it rains later. Isn't it more sensible to enjoy the sun while it lasts?

A third possibility is that you may be concerned that others won't receive your excitement with the same enthusiasm you feel. "After all," you might reason, "how could they possibly understand my joys? Better keep it inside me." This attitude assumes that if others don't understand they might undermine the importance a particular experience has for you. But why should someone else's negative attitude affect your actions? Aren't your feelings at least as important as the other person's?

Any of these reasons for holding back may be valid. At the same time, you ought to consider that you are also shutting off a vital dimension of your being. Your willingness to express positive emotions has to be a conscious choice. If in your judgment it will make *you* feel good, do it; you owe it to yourself to convey your feelings in a manner you consider appropriate.

Whether or not another person will be receptive to your enthusiasm is not as important as expressing your own feelings. And remember, if you dampen your spirits today because you're concerned about tomorrow, you miss out on two days.

If you listen to your inner voices, and respond honestly and judiciously, keeping in *mind that your objective is to profit from the business of living,* you can't miss.

15

Dealing with Your Depressions

Like any other enterprises, the business of living is cyclical —it has its peaks and valleys. During your peak periods the world looks bright, you are productive and happy with yourself, and you seem to enjoy life. Then there are the valleys—the down periods—when you feel dejected, apathetic, listless, and helpless. When you are in this state the world around you looks gloomy, and nothing seems to give you pleasure.

People in this "downer" frequently have an "I don't care" or a "What's the use" attitude, which only adds to their misery. Often it seems nothing and nobody can help them get out of it. Friends or relatives who offer their help are rejected. "Let me be miserable and beat my breast in peace," these people seem to say. "If you *really* want to help me, feel sorry for me and cry along with me."

Call it "being in the dumps," the "blues," a bad mood, or a depression—the feelings I am referring to are as common as a cold. They may last only a few hours, or they can linger for days, even weeks. These "blue" periods often come without warning, and they can happen to anyone.

Commercial firms try to anticipate their down periods, and take precautionary measures to protect themselves. During their peak times, they establish cash reserves from which they can draw when business is slow. They might also make prudent investments to provide them with a financial cushion when they need it. In short, they compensate for their down periods by making maximum use of their opportunities when business is good.

Unfortunately, this is where our analogy with the business of living ends. People do not have the capacity to save up good feelings and cash them in when they are depressed. Nor can they produce a surplus of positive experiences to hold them over during emotionally rough times. If these options were available to us, perhaps we could reduce the frequency or intensity of our "blue" periods.

While we lack this capacity, the fact is that there are ways of dealing with mild depressions—the kind most people experience in the course of living. Before I tell you how to manage these feelings, let's talk about what depression is and what brings on this condition.*

What Is Depression?

Viewing ourselves in the most simplistic way possible, there are two dimensions to the human being. First, there is the *thinking and feeling dimension.* Included in this part of us are all our private thoughts, desires, needs, wishes, wants, hopes, and emotional states. The second part is the *expressive and acting dimension.* This is the side of us which others see and react to.

For a person to be in tune with himself, these two parts of the individual, with the help of his judgment, have to work in harmony. An individual's judgment tells him when and how he can appropriately express his feelings, thoughts, and desires.

Now, suppose you have a thought or desire which you are not able to act on, or the actions you have to take are opposite from the way you feel. What happens is that you are, figuratively speaking, torn apart because one part of you is going one way while the other is doing nothing, or going in a different direction. As a result of splitting yourself apart, a void or empty feeling is

* The explanation that follows assumes that there is no physical basis for the depression. Severe depressions may be caused by an endocrinological imbalance. If this is a possibility, medical help should be sought.

created. *This void that is created is a feeling of frustration or depression. Frustration is a temporary obstacle* which stands in the way of achieving your objective, but *depression is a feeling of helplessness.*

Why are depressions so common? Because all of us are frequently required to do certain things we don't necessarily want to do. Or there are certain things we may want to do but can't. Or we may want certain things to happen, but, because we have no direct control and recourse, we are unable to do anything about our desires.

Many housewives are prone to depression. One of them is Rhoda, a twenty-eight-year-old, intelligent, attractive mother of two children. Rhoda hates housework. In one of our discussions, she lamented, "There are so many things I should be doing around the house, which I ignore. I find all kinds of excuses not to do what I know I must. Then the work piles up and I get depressed. I feel boxed into a situation I don't want to be in. I wasn't trained to be a housecleaner."

"So what are you doing about it?" I asked.

"I do as little as I can get away with. But because my heart isn't in it, I read and watch TV a lot. It's a horrible existence."

Then there is the rising lower-level executive, personified by Jay, who complains, "I work my tail off for my family. Every day I'm up early in the morning, catch my train, and put in a full day. I come home exhausted, and hardly have time for my wife and kids. What am I getting in return? I get depressed because I see no way out of this rat race. One day is like the next."

Just the other day, Dudley came into my office for his scheduled appointment. "I've been depressed all week," he said.

"What happened?"

"I've been after this account for the past month. I called on them regularly, and from all indications it looked like I would land it. I had good reason for anticipating making the sale, but at the last minute they decided to give their business to someone else."

"So your efforts didn't pan out. What did you do?"

"I was so depressed I couldn't do anything," he replied. "In fact, I couldn't do much all week. I felt no incentive to call on the accounts I have."

For many people the early or mid-forties is an age when depression seems to linger. Those I have met professionally view themselves critically, some of them for the first time. They look back to where they've been and reflect on what they have done with their lives; they are unhappy with their past. Then, when they look ahead and see little prospect for changing the course of their lives, they become terribly disillusioned. Here they are, caught between an unfulfilled past—all they can remember is working hard and denying themselves the pleasures of life—and an empty future that holds no more promise than the past. That's depressing. So what do they do? Many simply resign themselves to the belief that "That's life, and there is nothing I can do about it."

As a human being, I am also vulnerable to depressions—and I have my share of them. But I have also learned that there are some things I can do to snap out of them fairly quickly. Perhaps my approach will be helpful to you.

Overcoming Depression

The first question I ask myself when I am in a depressed state is, "What do I want that I am not getting?" Or "What do I feel, but somehow am not expressing?" These questions help me to *identify what is tearing me apart and what is causing the void.* After I have pinpointed the feeling or desire, I ask, "What can I do to help me fill this void?"

Action is the most constructive way to relieve depressing feelings. Simply thinking about what you feel or would like doesn't help; in fact, it adds to the depression. Action of some sort is the best way out of it.

For example, the housewife who hates housework and becomes depressed because she lets it slide, can *do* one of several things. She can stop thinking about it, and just get it done the best way she knows how. Or she can get a part-time job she enjoys, so she could pay for someone else to do her work. In the case of Rhoda, she took the first alternative. She decided to quit thinking about how much she hated housework, and to simply do what had to be done. Once she decided to take constructive action to help her overcome her feelings that she was negligent, her depression subsided.

A man in his forties, going through the "male menopause," might ask himself, "What can I do differently in the years ahead so that I enjoy life more than I have in the past?" In response to this question, Tim, who deprived himself practically all his adult life, developed a plan which he actually followed.

A machinist by trade, he worked hard to maintain a house and to support his wife and three children. A dedicated husband and father, as well as a conscientious worker, he did not resent his obligations, but he felt he had shortchanged himself during his first forty-five years of living. He never got around to signing up for the night classes he wanted to take just for fun, nor did he read many of the books he thought he would enjoy. And, finally, he had not done much traveling—his vacations were always short and not too far from home.

Tim first drew up a list of books he planned to read during the next few years. While not exhaustive, it was a start. He also signed up for a short course in practical psychology, a subject that had always fascinated him. Later he would decide on other courses—he thought about chess.

Tim and his wife also worked out a plan whereby they could see the States by car. Their first two-week vacation was scheduled for July. They opened a special savings account for that purpose, and he had seven months to save for their trip. The act of developing a plan for realizing some of his private dreams was enough to counteract his depression. When Tim started doing those things he promised himself, he came alive; the world looked brighter.

Sometimes we have feelings or desires which cannot be acted upon directly. A case in point would be a person who feels like quitting his job but for a variety of reasons is unable to. The void he feels, because he cannot do anything about his desires, is real and painful. How can this person relieve those tensions which grow with his dissatisfaction?

In such situations I would strongly recommend diverting activities. Adopting a hobby, exercising regularly, and taking frequent walks will undoubtedly help to relieve some of these tensions. The point is, *if you can't do anything specific about a situation, you must ask another question: "What can I do about myself so that my feelings of helplessness do not paralyze me?"* Again, activity of any type—some effort to mobilize yourself—is better than brooding about your condition.

Up to now I've talked about how failing to act on your feelings or desires can create depression. However, individuals can also *think* themselves into a depressed state. Thoughts about people and things, when they are not verbalized or expressed in some way, can precipitate this condition. Some of these thoughts may be about situations over which they have no control. For example, "If only I had done this instead of that," or "If my parents were more understanding, I wouldn't be in this predicament," or "Why aren't people more tolerant of each other?" or "Why did this catastrophe happen to me?"

These "if only" and "why" kinds of reflections serve no meaningful purpose. All they do is increase the intensity of your depression. "Why" questions may be a good place to start, but unless they lead to the next logical question, which is, "What can I do about it?" the whole thing becomes a fruitless intellectual exercise.

If you can't do anything about what other people have done or are doing, look for a way of relieving your anger or disappointment. A technique I have found useful is to *write my thoughts down on paper*. I may save them, throw them away, or send them to somebody. You can do the same. Get yourself a notebook. Whenever disturbing ideas crop up, write them down. It's not only a release, but you may be able to "see" your thoughts more clearly and, therefore, be more objective about them.

What about upsetting thoughts involving people with whom you have contact—like friends, relatives, and work associates: how do you handle them? I have known persons who think a great deal about what they would like to say, but don't. The more they think, the more upset, frustrated, or depressed they become.

My personal feeling is, if something about a person is disturbing you, make your thoughts known to the individual. Isn't that better than holding your thoughts in and allowing them to fester? If you are diplomatic about how to voice your ideas, chances are you will not hurt their feelings. As I said in an earlier chapter, mental masturbation is not emotionally healthy. Neither is mental constipation.

As an antidote to this common problem, I sometimes suggest to my clients that they ask themselves, "What is the worst thing that could happen if . . . ?" They often find that once they have faced the *worst* possible consequences—and they are often amazed to discover that they *can*—their worry diminishes substantially or disappears altogether.

More often than not, the worst doesn't happen. But even if it does, these individuals find resources in themselves that they never knew existed. The reward for trusting in their own strengths gives them more confidence the next time they are threatened by the paralysis of worrying about "What if . . . ?"

When people express their upsetting thoughts to those who matter to them they are often amazed at how much better they feel. As one woman told me, "I was reluctant to tell my boss what I thought about his treatment of me. I was afraid of how he would react. But I was really surprised when I did it. None of my fears were justified. Not only was *he* glad that I cleared the air with him, but *I* also felt relieved."

In Summary

—The more successful you are in *aligning your actions with your feelings, desires, and thoughts,* the less depressed you will become.

—When you feel depressed, ask yourself: "*What do I want* to happen that isn't, and *what can I do* about it?"

—Don't expend energy thinking about your depression; focus your attention on *doing something about it.*

—If you can't do anything about the desire, feeling, or thought that is causing your depression, *direct your thinking toward avenues that will prove personally productive.* Some action is better than nothing.

—When possible, *verbalize your thoughts,* rather than holding them in.

16

Don't Make Other People's Problems Yours

Several years ago a woman phoned me with the intention of making an appointment to discuss some personal problems. Initially it appeared to be a routine call. As it turned out, it wasn't.

"You were suggested to me by Dr. _____, and I'd like to see you, but I'm not sure I can."

"Why the hesitancy?"

"Well," she said, "I'm not sure. But let me ask you, are you Jewish?"

I couldn't quite understand what that had to do with making an appointment. I responded matter-of-factly to her question. "Yes, I am."

·"That's too bad," she said, "because now I can't come to see you."

"Why is that?"

"Because, to be perfectly honest with you, I hate Jews."

Somewhat taken aback, but still maintaining my professional composure, I replied, "Oh, I'm sorry about that."

"Did you say you're sorry?" she asked, surprised. "You mean you're not angry with me?"

"That's right," I said. "I am sorry you feel the way you do, and I'm not angry." (I lied about the angry part.)

"I don't understand your reaction. Why aren't you mad at me?"

Frankly, I was as surprised at my control as she was. But my

157

explanation to her was this: "Look, if you were to call your physician to complain about an ailment, would you expect him to be angry at you?"

"Of course not."

"This is no different. The fact that you hate Jews is *your* problem, and has little to do with me personally, since you don't even know me. If I reacted to your feelings with anger, I would be permitting your problems to dictate my behavior. There is no point in both of us being full of hate is there? Now, would you like to make an appointment or not?"

Shocked by my response, she made the appointment. I continued seeing her for about six months.

While my reactions to this woman were quite spontaneous, I learned a great deal from this incident; it brought to consciousness a very important principle for managing my life.

As far as this woman was concerned, I viewed her expressed hatred as a problem because it revealed a narrow-minded, bigoted attitude—a human weakness. When an individual exhibits weaknesses, shortcomings, or failings, he has, as far as I am concerned, problems. Symptoms of weaknesses include jealousy, impatience, rigidity, short temper, laziness, emotional dishonesty, and many others too numerous to mention. *They are problems because such weaknesses generally restrict an individual's personal freedom and create unnecessary barriers in relating to others.*

By emotionally reacting to another's weaknesses, particularly if your reactions cause you personal discomfort, you, in effect, reduce yourself to their level. That is, you allow their weaknesses to trigger off weaknesses in you. And in so doing you fall into a trap. You may, without really wanting to, become defensive, hostile, and unreasonable. All this happens when you make other people's problems yours.

A former student of mine adopted a phrase which he uses to remind him of this principle when he encounters rude waiters or waitresses, or when he is cut off by a speeding and careless driver, or in other situations which would normally cause him to blow up. He says to himself: "I'm not going to let you ruin my day." This phrase helps him to temper his reactions, and to handle, in a more reasonable manner, potentially disruptive day-to-day personal difficulties. He is now better able to take in stride quirks of people over whom he has no control, and to deal rationally with people he *can* influence. For example, he will report waitresses who are rude, rather than losing his self-control and thereby letting them ruin his day.

In the course of living you meet people whose values, standards, and styles of life are substantially different from yours. As long as they don't try to harm you and those things that are important to you, they are entitled to live their lives as they see fit. But, *when you interpret their actions as a personal affront, particularly if this is not their intention, you set yourself up for making their problems yours.* When you follow their lead, and allow others to influence your behavior and standards, you are incorporating their problems into your life-style.

Suppose you were employed in a job where one or two people were not, in your opinion, pulling their weight. If you used their behavior as an excuse for not putting out your best effort, you would, in effect, be saying, "Those weaknesses that are causing these people to shrug off their responsibilities are also my weaknesses." But the fact is that their reasons for defaulting have nothing to do with you. You are responsible for your own actions, not someone else's. If those around you want to goof off, that's their business. They are the ones who will have to live with the consequences that arise from their behavior.

When you adopt mediocre standards just because "everyone else is," you create inner conflicts for yourself. Remember, you've got your own life to lead. When you look in the mirror, you see yourself, not someone else. How do *you* feel about your performance when it is mediocre? Can you look at yourself with pride? If others want to hurt themselves, that's *their* choice. But that is no reason to blindly follow their decisions; make your own choices.

If you allow them to, others will pressure you into adopting their weaknesses so that you do things which are not right for you. Let's look at a couple of examples:

The first involves a teen-ager who complained to me that her mother was constantly "bitchy." According to this seven-teen-year-old girl, her mother got angry and found fault with anything and everything she did or didn't do. Regardless of how small the problem, her mother griped incessantly about it.

"What specifically is she bitchy about?"

"Usually it's about things I don't do around the house. Some-times she gets mad at the way I do things."

"How do you react to her bitchiness?"

"I'm bitchy in return."

"Do you like being that way?"

"No," she said, "I hate myself."

When I pointed out that she allowed her mother's problem (being bitchy) to become her problem (being bitchy in return), she was able to see that she was displaying the same qualities she was criticizing. "Okay," I said, "if you don't like yourself when you act bitchy toward your mother, what actions would make you feel good?"

She decided that regardless of her mother's reactions she would do the best job she could—a job she would be proud of. She reasoned that if she herself could be pleased with the quality and quantity of her domestic efforts, she would at least have some satisfactions. As expected, when she followed through on her plan, her mother became considerably less bitchy and more tolerable. But, more important, because the girl refused to fall into the trap, she felt better about herself.

The second example came to my attention recently. Marv is a twenty-seven-year-old married man with two children. He has been employed by the same company since graduating from college. When he came to me he expressed his dissatisfaction with his job for the past three years. Worse than that, he wasn't certain whether he was on a career road that would make him happy.

I thought the logical first step would be to explore some alternative career avenues. After talking about his likes, dislikes, and abilities, we decided on two options he might investigate. His assignment was to talk with people in these fields so he could determine what the opportunities might be. When he left me he was enthusiastic and eager to embark on this project.

The following week he entered my office looking as if the world had come to an end. "This was the worst week I have had in a long time," he told me.

"What made it so?"

"I talked to my father, and told him I was seriously thinking of changing jobs and possibly my career. Without waiting for an explanation, he told me I was a damn fool. He also told me to quit behaving like a child. He reminded me of my obligations to my family, and said that I ought to shape up and be a responsible adult."

"And what was your reaction?"

"I'm confused, and not at all sure that I want to change anything now."

We talked about his father. Marv's father had been a civil-service employee for thirty years, and progressed to a reasonably respectable position. Over the years his father instilled in Marv the notion that a responsible person holds on to one job and grows with the company. As far as he was concerned, anyone who did not follow this formula for building a career was irresponsible. Since Marv's decision to investigate new opportunities threatened his father's image of how a responsible person should act, he had lashed out at his son.

"How do you feel about your dad's attitude?" I asked.

"It's narrow-minded," he replied, "but it worked for him in a limited way. Dad was content, but he also rejected several outstanding offers."

"But you've accepted his narrow thinking, and as a result it's restricting your own development. Don't you see," I explained, "by adopting your dad's philosophy, which you admit has limited his own career growth, you have made his problems yours. He had his reasons or excuses for doing what he did, which was right for him. But does that mean they have to be right for you?"

"If he's been successful, what is his problem?"

"I don't know, and it doesn't matter," I replied. "The point is that you have as much right to your views as he does to his. And if you try to live your life by his standards, which you do not share, you are permitting his biases and attitudes to create emotional turmoil within you."

"It seems," Marv replied, "I've been doing this all my life. I used to exaggerate and lie just to please him. I would tell him what I thought he wanted to hear, rather than what was actually true. Does that make sense?"

"Isn't it conceivable that his ideas of a 'good' son could be distorted? If you felt the pressure to lie in order to conform to his image of what a 'good' son should be, you were, even then, making his problems yours."

Marv seemed to understand and decided to pursue his career investigation on a full scale, and not allow his father's "problems" to rub off on him. He also decided to develop standards *he* could live with.

A corollary to the major principle I've been discussing is: *Don't permit others to force you into doing things which will cause you to dislike yourself.* Because others have their own desires which they strive to satisfy, they may pressure you to do things that are not in your best interest. These pressures, which come in many forms, must be weighed carefully.

A friend of mine in the field of market research told me that he learned this principle the hard way. When he first formed his organization his clients pressed him to conduct studies in less time than he felt was possible. In order to get the business, he accepted the assignments in spite of the unreasonable deadlines. Of course, he could not deliver the quality of work that met his standards. Not only was he dissatisfied with himself, but his impatient clients were also displeased with his work.

It didn't take my friend long to realize that his clients' impatience was *their* problem, and by yielding to it he was causing problems for himself. Now, when clients ask him to conduct a study in less time than he believes is reasonable, he tells them so. Even when they threaten to take their business elsewhere, he maintains his position. He explains that he would do them an injustice by rushing the job. As it turns out, he loses very little business, and the clients he does lose are not worth having—not at the price of his professional integrity.

In your relationships with people, you can quickly determine whether you are making someone else's problems yours. Just ask yourself, *"Do I feel terribly uncomfortable or uneasy because of what this person wants me to do?"* If your answer is yes, I would suggest that you think about the actions you intend to take before doing things you'll be sorry for later. Don't allow others to make you feel guilty about your decisions. To repeat a statement I've made several times before, you have a right to lead your own life and to conduct your business according to your own ideals.

There are, of course, situations where others do in fact make their problems yours. A case in point is when someone spreads an unfounded rumor about you. Or when a person whom you have to work with holds a personal grudge against you. Under circumstances where you are the object of such attacks you have three choices. First, you can *ignore the individual,* and go about your business. Second, you can *confront the person and attempt to resolve the difficulty.* And, finally, you can *ask an interested third party to serve as an intermediary* in resolving the conflict.

Another common situation where others make their problem yours is, unfortunately, unavoidable. For example, suppose a friend promises to help you on a particular project, but at the last minute backs out of it. His reasons, excuses, or personal problems are immaterial. The point is that you are stuck because he hasn't come through.

All you can do in those circumstances is to *accept it, do the best you can, and don't be too quick to count on him again.* Admittedly he has created problems for you, but being nasty about it doesn't solve *your* problem. Looking for a solution is more profitable than dissipating your energies and thereby increasing your problems.

Part 5

IF YOU WANT
A PARTNER

17

The Business of Marriage

Some companies or corporations may choose to form a partnership or to merge with another business when they feel they can benefit from such a relationship. Their decision is based upon some objective analysis of their potential mutual gains.

This is not true when marital partnerships are formed. The forces that attract two people to each other are based largely upon the feelings that exist between them. Their decision to marry is more emotional than logical. Romance seems to overpower reason when choosing a mate. It is probably the only time in our life when we sign a lifelong binding contract without the aid of a competent attorney.

Though some couples retain a lawyer to negotiate a marital contract, this is neither a common practice nor one that I would advocate. The compelling role emotions play in *establishing* a union cannot be underestimated. But these powerful feelings alone are insufficient to *sustain* a marriage. A marital partnership has to weather many storms, and the couple must be able to adapt to the numerous changes that inevitably come. Unless the initial attracting forces are fortified with more durable bonds, the relationship deteriorates.

Deterioration is not necessarily sudden. It can be a gradual process, which begins with each or both partners' failure to fully understand what they are really contracting for when they take their marriage vows and sign the agreement. Most are too en-

167

chanted by their emotions to realize what personal obligations they are implicitly agreeing upon. Failing to understand their commitments, obviously they can't honor them. Granted, these romantic blind spots are common to couples who are about to take the plunge. But when they marry they face the need to discover the significance of their contract and then honor it.

Unfortunately, many people do not actively respond to this challenge because they don't view it as such. To these individuals marriage is an institution they learn to tolerate. They stumble along and become increasingly disillusioned with each other as well as with the relationship. What began as a beautiful romance disintegrates into a convenient, but not very pleasant, arrangement.

While this is the fate of a large percentage of marital partnerships, it need not be that way. I believe that more couples would profit from their marital venture if they approached it with the seriousness and sincerity it rightly deserves. If marriage were viewed as an extension of a person's career (in the business of living) it would achieve a more significant status.

But before we get into some practical suggestions for building a healthy marital relationship, let me define my concept of marriage. *The "business" of marriage is a continual mutual investment venture of two people who want and expect from this union certain unique dividends they cannot attain through any other relationship.* Probably the most difficult and complicated relationship to manage, marriage requires emotional, intellectual, physical/sexual, and financial investments.

To develop a mutually profitable venture, both parties must give serious thought to each of the following issues:

1. They must define for themselves *what dividends they want from this union.* They have to determine what they want and need from their partner that they couldn't achieve either on their own or through some other non-marital relationship.

2. They have to seriously consider *what specific investments*

are required to yield these dividends. They must then commit themselves to making these investments.

3. They must make every effort to both *protect and capitalize on their investments.*

4. Finally, they must appreciate the fact that *marriage does not destroy each partner's individuality.* Marriage is a union of two individuals with unique experiences, abilities, problems, and needs.

I will now elaborate on the first three points. The fourth will be discussed in the next chapter.

What Are the Potential Dividends?

When a person accepts a job he generally knows, or at least has thought about, what he wants to get out of it. In addition to the financial returns he expects for his efforts, he also hopes to gain some personal satisfaction from doing a good job. Similarly, when two people form a business partnership they do so on the assumption that they can complement each other. By combining their efforts and individual skills, they believe they can be more successful than if each functioned independently.

What about the potential benefits or dividends of marriage? Few if any other relationships offer greater opportunities for personal-emotional satisfactions than that entered into by two people who are committed to bringing out the best in each other.

As co-founders and co-directors of a self-created enterprise, a husband and wife have unique challenges. If they have children, they can be instrumental in directing the activities and shaping the lives of people who need guidance and leadership. They are responsible for making decisions which can either destroy or help develop those who depend upon them. Their actions and words can make a profound difference in each of their lives, as well as in the lives of people they bring into this world. What other relationship or position can provide you with an opportunity to be this important?

Aside from these general benefits, I know of no other relationship that can give you the same kind of freedom to be yourself, and to enjoy a sincere, deep, and honest friendship. Those couples who are truly happily married—and I have met many—describe their relationship as *one based upon true friendship*—it is noncompetitive and nonjudgmental. They are willing to accept those weaknesses and idiosyncrasies in each other that no one else will put up with. They see each other before and after they put on their public masks, but that doesn't seem to affect their basic relationship. Each of these partners has a sincere interest in the other's well-being; they achieve satisfaction by pleasing their spouse (without, of course, sacrificing their own values).

In a world where each of us is constantly being judged, put to the test, rewarded for our performance, as well as punished or criticized when we do not produce, it is good to know that someone—a special person—is committed to your well-being. It is satisfying to feel that this person will accept you, regardless of your day-to-day output, economic and marketing conditions, mood changes, and health, that there is a person with whom you can "let your hair down." And it is a source of strength and encouragement to share your personal struggles with someone who cares about the *total* you, and not just the productive you.

There is also a sense of security in knowing that you have a companion who cares enough to stand by you even when others will not. Here is a person who is willing to give himself or herself to you physically and emotionally without strings attached. Who else but a wholly committed mate will support you when you need it most?

Then, of course, there is romantic love—that intangible feeling that drew you and your spouse together in the first place. This romance deepens and strengthens only if it is an outgrowth of a solid relationship.

What do you want from your marriage that you can't get from any other relationship? It would be a worthwhile project for you and your spouse to sit down, during a quiet period, and list your individual desires. That is, *what dividends do you want from your relationship?* After both of you have made your lists, discuss them. It may take several hours, but the experience will be rewarding and certainly enlightening.

What You Need to Invest

Those who have been successful in the marriage venture will attest that the dividends I've mentioned can be realized. But to do so, you obviously have to make substantial investments. Nothing of value is obtained inexpensively and without sincere effort. The commitment you want from your mate has to be earned. Since no other relationship I know of is more demanding and complex than marriage, your investments will need to be at least as great as you might expect to make in a responsible job.

Probably the single most important investment necessary to make your marriage succeed is time. The number of hours you spend with your spouse is not the important issue: quality is what really counts. This means that you have to convey the feeling that you really care. Your partner has to feel your presence and your emotional support whether or not you are physically together. This feeling can be conveyed through *the three essential ingredients for building a healthy relationship: mutual love, respect, and trust.*

Love. One of the most abused words in the English language is "love." As I conceive it, there are two dimensions to love—it is both an *emotion* and an *attitude.*

The loving *emotion* cannot be defined since the same word is used to express different feelings of affection. The love you may feel for a spouse is not the same as that which you feel for a child, parent, brother (or sister), or friend. So, when you say "I love you" to each of them you are expressing a strong positive emotion, but the quality of this feeling cannot be described.

However, the loving *attitude* can be defined. It is *an individual's desire and commitment to do or say those things, and to create an environment, which bring out the best in the person he loves.* This attitude, in my opinion, is a basic requirement for all genuine loving relationships. It can be expressed in many ways.

Any of these gestures, for example, would convey this attitude: A call during the day: "How are you? How are things going? Everything under control?" Or, when you are together, "Anything I can do to help you?" Or any spontaneous act that says, in effect, "I appreciate you and empathize with your problems, and I am willing to extend myself to ease your burden."

Either spouse can demonstrate his love by making things more comfortable for the other, encouraging each other when encouragement is needed, and listening to gripes as well as sharing joys and successes.

Both partners express loving attitudes when each looks out for the other's best interests; that's the only way they can protect their own interests. By being encouraging, and by helping each other cope with the normal stresses of life, as well as their individual weaknesses, each partner brings out the best in the other.

How you go about achieving this objective is an individual matter; the same set of actions may bring out the best in one person and the worst in another. An example of how this is possible was related to me recently by a patient. Clara described her former husband as "a gentle, unselfish, and kind person who gave me everything I asked for. He rarely raised his voice, and never rejected my requests or demands. The more I demanded from him, the more I got. When I would be nasty and mean to him, he just kept quiet and took it. He was too good to be real."

"Sounds like he was a great guy," I said. "Why did you divorce him?"

"I couldn't stand it any more," she replied. "I was becoming a demanding, spoiled, nagging bitch. I asked him to stop being so overly kind, and to put his foot down. But he said he couldn't because he loved me too much. The more he loved me the more I hated what I was turning into. His love was not the kind I needed. So I filed for divorce."

Her husband's kindness and generosity were probably motivated by emotional love, but he failed to consider *her* needs. Even though he saw her turn into a shrew, he persisted in his behavior because it made *him* feel good. His loving attitude was more self-serving than spouse-oriented. If he *really* loved her he would not have continued doing those things that brought out the worst in her.

Which brings us to the next ingredient for building a healthy marital partnership:

Respect. You extend respect to another person when you consider his feelings, desires, and needs. This means, of course, that you must become aware of them, which is really the first step in building a marriage. Couples who have a healthy marital partnership tend to view their relationship as a *mutual teaching adventure*—each learns from the other. They learn, among other things, about each other's emotional and physical requirements and the value their partner places on each one. Each implicitly adopts the attitude that "your feelings, opinions, ideas and desires regarding problems that affect you and me as individuals, as well as our partnership, are important to me. I think about what you have to say and what you want."

Successfully married couples also learn appropriate methods of responding to their partner's needs. A husband, for example, learns when his wife, who blows up at something or other, wants to be left alone and when she wants to be pampered. A wife learns when her husband, who has had difficulties at work, needs to be listened to and when he requires advice. They both learn to pick up cues regarding each other's sexual inclinations and then respond accordingly.

A question I am frequently asked is, "Do I have to respond favorably to every request my wife [or husband] makes of me?" Learning to discern the vital from the not so important needs or desires is a matter of judgment. To reduce some of the guess-work, a couple might do well to agree on one assumption which is: *I would not ask you to do anything which is distasteful to you unless it was extremely important to me.* If you are reluctant to honor my request, it is at least worthy of discussion.

Implied in this agreement is a question each partner must answer for himself: "Are my reasons for not wanting to grant the request sufficiently strong to hurt my spouse's feelings?" This question forces a person to weigh the relative importance of two competing desires (his and hers). Two examples will clarify this point.

Hilda has three small children and is a dedicated housewife. She practically begged Tom to watch the children for a half-hour after he came home from work so she could rest before serving dinner. "I work hard all day too," he complained, "and I also want to relax." His continual failure to respect her needs bred resentment on her part, which affected their evening's relationship.

I asked Tom if he *ever* watched the children as his wife requested. "Several times," he said.

"And how was your wife's disposition when you did?"

"Great. I wish she could be that way all the time."

"It seems to me," I said, "that you're missing a good deal. If all you have to give is a half-hour in return for three hours of good company, you can't afford to pass that up. If you want, you can even relax after dinner."

He thought about it and said, "I'll try it for a week to see what happens." The following session he and his wife reported that they had enjoyed a good week together. Once he realized that her needs prior to dinnertime were more important than his, he willingly assumed the responsibility of taking care of the children for that period.

Another example: A friend of mine tentatively accepted an invitation to go on a fishing trip with two of his associates. When he told his wife about it, she reminded him that on the Saturday of that weekend she was being installed as president of the local women's club. It was a dinner affair and husbands had been invited. He had forgotten about it, but the trip was difficult to pass up. Betty told him that this was very important to her, and that she would like him to be present. He turned down the fishing invitation because "I could always make it another time, but for Betty this is a rare occasion."

Respect is also demonstrated when a couple is receptive to each other's thoughts and perceptions. Assuming you married your partner because that person has certain unique qualities and interests that can complement yours, doesn't it make sense to acknowledge and benefit from his virtues rather than ignore them? Couples who respect each other discover all kinds of intellectual, social, and other skills that each possesses.

Valuing each other's areas of expertise, they use each other as resources on those matters in which each needs help. *It's not a matter of what is a "woman's job" or what is a "man's job." Rather, it's a question of who is best equipped and has the most time to do the best job possible.* That's what a partnership based on respect is all about.

Your spouse can also be an excellent source of feedback. He or she can tell you how you came across to others. You can look to each other for help in improving your behavior and attitudes. As one happily married husband expressed it, "My wife tells me things about myself nobody else would. And I listen to her because I trust her judgment."

Trust. Mutual trust is the third and final ingredient necessary for a successful marital partnership. *A trusting relationship demands that each spouse agree to the assumption, "You would not do anything to deliberately hurt me."* It is important to make this agreement because husbands and wives frequently get into arguments about matters of mutual concern. During these disagreements each may say things purely out of anger. If these comments are taken literally and personally they can create insurmountable walls between you and your spouse.

To develop a climate of trust you must begin by being

trustworthy yourself. Here are some questions you might ask yourself which will help you evaluate to what degree you are fulfilling your end of the bargain:

1. Do I seriously consider important and place value on what my partner says, even when his or her ideas do not agree with mine?
2. Do I sense my partner's need for help in resolving his or her personal problems? And do I willingly offer whatever help I can give?
3. Do I defend my spouse against adverse or unreasonable criticism which may be leveled at him or her by in-laws, friends, or other people?
4. Do I maintain those confidences he or she shares with me?
5. Do I keep most of those promises I made to him or her?
6. Do I permit outsiders to negatively influence my attitude and behavior toward my partner?
7. Do I embarrass my partner in front of other people?
8. Do I fail to inquire about my partner's side of an issue when there are two sides?
9. Does my partner fail to make requests of me because I frequently reject him or her?
10. Do I frequently make my partner feel he or she has to be on guard in my presence?

A "yes" response to the first five questions and a "no" response to the second five would strongly suggest that you have the basic requirements for being a trustworthy spouse. If your partner's responses are also perfect, the two of you could have written this chapter.

There is no limit to how much a couple can invest in each other. The nature of their investments will vary. What is important, however, is that each partner take a sincere interest in their marital venture and that both do what they can to protect and capitalize on their investments. Both partners have much to lose by not cooperating, and a great deal to gain by giving unselfishly to the other.

I've heard it said that marriage is a 50-50 relationship. That, frankly, doesn't make sense because it suggests that both spouses are holding back half of what they are capable of giving. A more reasonable position is that it is a 100-100 relationship. When *both* partners give 100 per cent of themselves each also receives all of what the other has to offer. You can't ask for more than that.

Protecting and Capitalizing on Your Investments

Prior to marriage men and women expend considerable effort to "make the sale." During this courting period each party puts the best foot forward. They are cordial as well as considerate toward each other, and extend themselves to please their partner-to-be. They make all kinds of promises, either implied or explicit, and they give the impression that the "product" they are selling is the best on the market.

Frankly, I'm all for presenting oneself in a favorable light, provided one does not misrepresent oneself. That's just good business. But as any successful salesman will tell you, making the sale is relatively easy. What is difficult is keeping the customer happy so he is neither vulnerable to nor actively seeks out competing suppliers. Having made a sale, the good salesman needs to be conscientious about servicing his account.

In marriage you can offer two levels of services: (1) "basic maintenance" and (2) "account building."

Basic Maintenance Services. In an effort to protect your investments it is essential that you perform certain duties and functions required of any partner—those aimed at keeping your spouse from becoming dissatisfied with you and the relationship. In effect, both partners do what is required of them—nothing more nor less. Because they fulfill each other's minimum expectations, usually of a tangible nature, neither spouse can fault the other.

I have heard wives say: "My husband is a good man. He earns a nice living, we live in a nice house, we go on a vacation every year, he doesn't forget my birthday or our anniversary, we go out from time to time, and our sexual relations aren't too bad. What else can you expect?"

"Are you happy?" I ask.

"I'm not unhappy. It could be worse."

Husbands whose wives function primarily on this "maintenance" level have this to say about their wives: "She's a good woman. She keeps a clean house, has dinner ready when I get home, takes care of the kids, looks nice when we go out, doesn't refuse me when I want sex, and doesn't make too many demands on me. What else can you ask for?"

"Are you happy?"

"I'm not unhappy; it could be worse."

Yes, I think to myself, it could be worse. But it also could be better.

Both descriptions sound like they are made by people who have settled into a rut, not a relationship. Many partnerships remain on this level for many years, neither party realizing that they are stunting each other's growth. Other relationships that remain on this basic level eventually falter and deteriorate into a convenient arrangement. In many instances one or both partners seek greener pastures. That, unfortunately, is one of the penalties of passively protecting your investments. The alternative is to actively build and capitalize on them.

Account-building Services. The creative salesman may start out with small accounts, but his objective is to build and expand them. He is an idea person, constantly on the lookout for new opportunities to serve his customers. He is sensitive to their growing as well as current needs. He searches for ways in which he can become more important to them.

Why the effort? Because it is generally more fun to build

than to break new ground. Also, it is more challenging and gratifying to help a company grow, and to develop with the organization, than to chase new accounts. Once he makes a sale, a salesman would be foolish not to cultivate that account.

Similarly, couples who are dedicated to enriching rather than simply maintaining their marriage consciously search for ways of "turning on" their partner. They are committed to making each other happy and to building a solid, meaningful relationship. I have met my fair share of couples who work at enriching their marriage. A composite picture of the attitudes and behavior exhibited by such partners is revealed in the following hypothetical interview.

"What keeps your marriage vibrant and vital? How do you keep it from becoming stale?"

He: I think it has to do with our attitudes toward each other. My wife makes me feel that I'm the most important person in her life. Take the other day, for example. I came home from a particularly rough day at work, and it apparently showed on my face. Jean suggested that, rather than having dinner with the children, we feed them first and have a quiet meal by ourselves later in the evening. That's exactly what we did, and it was great.

She: It works both ways. There are many times when I've had an absolutely rotten day—you know, the kind of day where nothing goes right. Somehow Bill senses it, and he suggests we go out to dinner. Or he may bring home flowers. Sometimes he suggests that we go for a walk or take a ride. I never know what he'll come up with—it's something I don't expect. But one thing I can be sure of is that he thinks of ways to brighten my day. And do you know what? He succeeds most of the time.

He: Maybe it's being selfish, but when I succeed in making Jean feel good she's much better company. By helping her I also benefit.

She: That's just about the way I feel. All it takes is a few minutes of my day to ask myself: "What would Bill like? What would please him?" It's not that much of an effort to be thoughtful, you know.

"What about when he comes home? Do you still have things to talk about even after fifteen years of marriage?"

She: Oh, sure. He tells me about the things that are going on at work—the problems as well as some of the crazy things that happen. It's almost as if I'm right there with him. And when he shares his problems with me I feel important when I can say or do anything to help him. I'm not merely a housekeeper, I'm his associate.

He: Jean is easy to talk to because she listens, just as I do when she tells me about some of the things that go on at home. I'm not just referring to problems. She also talks to me about the fun things that go on during the day. I don't ever feel that I'm working just to pay bills. I'm as much a part of this house as she is.

"I suppose you have many interests in common?"

He: Actually, we have very few of the same interests. Jean likes to play bridge and tennis, but I don't. I enjoy fishing and bowling once a week but these activities don't interest her. We don't even enjoy reading the same books.

She: But that doesn't mean anything. For example, I'll play bridge maybe once a week and Bill goes bowling on his night. He's interested in hearing about my good times, just as I enjoy hearing him tell about his evening. And, on occasion, if I ask him to play bridge when we have company, he does. And when he asks me, I go along with his idea to go bowling. It's fun when we go together, even though it isn't my favorite sport.

It's strange how it works out. Bill doesn't like to go

shopping. But when I ask him, he'll go with me and we have a good time together. Maybe that's the whole secret. *We accommodate each other.*

"So, what you're saying is that you encourage each other to pursue your individual interests. And, on occasion, both of you will participate in your spouse's interests, but not as vigorously."

She: That's it exactly. I remember about two years ago I told Bill that I was bored with just being a housewife. We talked about it, and he suggested that I take a course. I finally decided on astronomy. That subject always interested me. Since then I've taken other subjects—not for a degree, but for fun.

He: When Jean studied she shared some of her new knowledge with me, and I learned, too. In fact, I helped her study for her exams. I wasn't interested enough to sit through a whole course, but I learned through Jean.

She: I don't necessarily expect him to help me, but he does it. In the same way he does many other spontaneous things for me which I don't expect. I suppose he enjoys doing things for me as much as I like to please him.

"Can you maintain an exciting sexual relationship after these many years?"

She: It gets better with time. Bill makes me feel desirable, and I in turn try to keep myself appealing.

He: She sure does. And, on occasion, when I feel we are drifting apart, I'll suggest we take a weekend and go to a motel to become reacquainted. Those weekends are great for revitalizing a marriage. We find new and exciting ways to enjoy each other's company. Not just sexually, either.

She: We experiment and try things we haven't done before

and we do things we normally wouldn't do at home. But when we return, we are recharged.

"One final question. Do you ever argue?"

He: Of course. But I think a better term would be discuss. There are some things we don't agree on, but my wife has her reasons for feeling one way, and I have mine for feeling another. We present our views, and talk it out until we reach some workable agreement.

She: We have a rule of never going to bed angry at each other. One time we talked until three in the morning before we resolved our differences.

"Sounds to me like you've got a relationship based on love, respect, and trust."

He and she: That's it in a nutshell.

18

What Marriage Is Not

Getting married is easy. Staying married is difficult. And remaining happily married is a full-time challenge met by relatively few people.

The mortality rate of marital partnerships is high. So are the emotional and financial costs that accompany divorces. The emotional price for couples who, despite their misery, remain married cannot be calculated. In the business of living one can hardly afford the drain of a nonproductive and destructive relationship. Yet such partnerships may and often do exist for many years.

No single reason can explain all marital failures. However, I am convinced that many marriages that go on the rocks do so because one or both parties enter the relationship with false assumptions. One of my preliminary questions when I see a couple for counseling is, "How long have you been having difficulties?" I am amazed at the number of people whose response is, "As far back as I can remember," or "Practically from the first day we were married."

When I ask how they got along before they were married, most people I see say that their relationship was great, that's why they got married. They talk about all the good times and fun they had together. But they explain that "it's different when you marry."

It is almost as if these people are saying that a marital

relationship is governed by a different set of rules and attitudes than a nonmarital relationship. Why a legal document—the marriage license—should influence people's basic attitudes toward each other is a difficult and complex question, with no easy answer. But it is usually clear to me in these situations that one or both spouses fail to view their marriage as a partnership.

In an effective partnership both parties must assume that *they are important to each other* in achieving their own as well as their common needs and objectives. They must assume that *this has to be an individual as well as a team effort.* They must assume that *only when they are united toward achieving common goals can they hope to achieve their own goals better.* And finally, by focusing on their goals, effective partners are encouraged to *fight the problems they encounter rather than each other.*

On the other hand, in the problem marriages I have seen and dealt with, the attitudes expressed (either verbally or in action) are:

1. My spouse is a possession who must be controlled and kept in her or his place.
2. My spouse is a competitor or adversary whom I must conquer.
3. I need to make sacrifices and give up my individuality when I am married.

Any one or combination of these assumptions can prove disastrous in building and developing a mutually profitable marital partnership. In this chapter I would like to examine these assumptions and suggest alternative ways of viewing your relationship.

A Spouse Is Not a Possession

Too often people forget that *marriage is a union of two independent and unique individuals.* Do they lose their individuality the moment they marry? Is the marriage certificate a contract of ownership? The answer to both questions is a resounding *no*.

When you own something you normally treat the object you purchased as a functional possession with certain prescribed roles. In marriages based on this assumption, one person takes on the role of "purchaser." For the sake of discussion, let us say it is the husband (although it could also be the wife). Such husbands typically assume the job of "breadwinner," while the wife is viewed as the hired domestic help. The "hired help" is told, in effect, "You are my property. Your role is to serve me. Your opinions and desires don't matter. Just do what you're supposed to do and you will be taken care of."

Since the "purchaser" is paying the "salary" and all the upkeep, he feels perfectly justified in demanding obedience. Because he views his wife as a subservient and relatively insignificant possession, he plays the dominant role in making decisions and in determining his wife's, as well as the entire family's, activities. A husband who subjugates his wife to this role fosters a childlike dependency and thus maintains control over his spouse.

These attitudes are very much like those of autocratic supervisors I have known. Such managers fail to involve their key personnel in departmental decisions. They assume their employees are incapable of thinking for themselves, and are not particularly interested in the responsibility of making decisions. Autocratic managers fail to give their subordinates credit for having initiative or ideas worth considering. The only ideas that matter are theirs, and the job of their personnel is to do as they are told. So, those subordinates wind up having responsibility without appropriate authority.

Employees treated in this way retaliate by doing only what they must in order to keep their jobs. They do not extend themselves in any form. Rather, they learn to protect their security by becoming "yes men." Since they feel emotionally divorced from their work and the company that employs them, they find their satisfactions elsewhere. And what about the manager? He also loses out because he limits his input and fails to develop subordinates who can help him grow. After all, what can he expect from people who are treated as if they were things?

This analogy is useful—as far as it goes. In a business, of course, no matter how good or sympathetic a manager is to his subordinates, they are still his subordinates. In a productive marriage, on the other hand, the roles of "manager" and "subordinate" may change, depending on the problem at hand and who is more capable of dealing with it. The point is, are both partners willing and able to treat each other with the openmindedness and receptivity that both deserve?

When the answer to this question is no, problems arise.

For example, a wife who passively accepts a subservient role and defines her value as a person according to her spouse's standards resigns herself to a prescribed, limited function. Because she does not recognize any other value to her being, she follows in her husband's shadow. The independence and individuality she had when she married is gone, and she becomes simply a tool for her spouse. She hesitates to stand up for herself, nor does she make it clear that she is an important person who deserves to be treated accordingly.

Husbands of wives who have allowed themselves to remain in this self-created trap are not particularly happy with this arrangement. Will's complaint to me is typical. "My wife is a weak, dependent, uninteresting, and unstimulating woman. I don't enjoy her company any more, and I haven't from the time we were married. It's like being married to a kid. She doesn't have opinions about anything. I've got to make all the decisions."

"Is that why you've been having this affair with Judy?" I asked.

"Pat [his wife] drove me to it. At first I put in more time at the office. I found every possible excuse not to come home. There was nothing to look forward to. Then I met Judy. She made me feel alive. We could discuss things, and she would even disagree with me. She knew what she wanted from life and went after it."

"And what about your wife, Will, isn't she interesting?"

"She was before we married. But I don't know what happened. It's almost like her brain turned off. We didn't discuss anything. I told her what I wanted and she just followed my wishes like a trained dog. You wouldn't want to be married to someone like that, would you?"

Of course, Will didn't recognize that he was the trainer, and that he expected his wife to assume this role. He forced her into a dependent trap and then faulted her for walking into it.

When I talked with Pat, I got the other side of the picture. "I didn't want to lose him," she said. "But when I finally realized that he was using me, I became resentful and angry."

"When did you first notice this?" I asked.

"About ten years ago." (They've been married for fifteen years.)

"What did you do about it?"

"Nothing. I still didn't want to lose him, and I thought that being married to him was better than being divorced. Anyway, we had two children, so what was I supposed to do?"

"What did you do?"

"I just decided that I wouldn't have much to do with him. At first I became depressed and pouted. Then I got involved with the house, kids, P.T.A., and neighbors. But the more involved I got, the more resentment I felt toward Will. After a while I wouldn't even go to bed with him. And it seemed that he didn't care."

"It seems like you had a cold war going on between you," I said.

"Worse than that," Pat replied. "I wanted to hurt him and get back at him for the pain he caused me. After a while we couldn't talk civilly to each other. Our arguments became vicious. All we wanted to do was destroy each other."

"Did that help?" I asked.

"No. It just made things worse. We finally stopped talking to each other. We went our separate ways. I would have dinner ready for him when he came home, and that was maybe once or twice a week. I would also do his laundry and anything else that needed to be done. But I couldn't take it any more. When I threatened divorce, and actually saw an attorney, he decided that we better get help."

The dominant and overbearing spouse could be either the husband or the wife. The wife who assumes this role views her husband as a Casper Milquetoast who does nothing more than respond to his wife's wishes: "Yes, dear, anything you say, dear," is his major form of conversation—anything to please and not to make waves.

Those spouses who allow themselves to be dominated and to be treated as a possession have two options. First, they can take it, and in so doing sink further into themselves. But this reaction results in their feeling less and less worthwhile. Their partner's feelings that they have an undesirable spouse are only reinforced.

The other option, once they realize that they have been "taken," is to stand up for themselves and *establish a new set of rules* for a better working relationship. A partner who has been treated like an object must show her or his teeth, and make it known that she will not tolerate this treatment. In so doing she gains her partner's attention, which is how all changes begin. Of course, when their spouses do not respond to their attention-getting methods, they must be prepared to back up threats with action—seeking legal help and divorce may be inevitable. But isn't it better to lose a partner than to lose yourself? When you lose yourself, what have you got left?

Marriage Is Not Competitive

Competition has no place in a partnership. When you compete, you attempt to demonstrate how much better you are than someone else. The nature of competition is that one person wins and another loses. When two people are working toward common objectives, what value is gained by proving the other person inferior?

Spouses who compete with one another are saying, in effect, "Look at me, I have chosen a partner who is less adequate than I am." If that is what comes across, what does that say about the person who wins? To me it says that the winner's judgment is not very good. After all, what kind of person would choose an inferior teammate?

Couples who have a competitive relationship, as opposed to a mutually supportive one, view their partners as adversaries. And, as is so often the case, they try to "beat" each other or "put down" their opponent. They do anything within reason to draw attention away from their opponent and toward themselves. If couples battle each other so that one person comes out on top, that can only do one thing to the partnership—weaken it.

To form a strong union, both partners must first find their *own* individual areas of interest and expertise which can give them the personal satisfaction they need. They must also *acknowledge, support, and benefit from each other's abilities and positive qualities.* In short, each must allow the other to have the limelight in his own area of confidence; and each be willing to take a back seat when his partner's subject is being discussed.

Let's look at two contrasting examples:

Harvey continually talks down to his wife Sharon, particularly in front of others. When I asked Harvey what initially attracted him to his wife, he said: "She was beautiful, independent, and strong-willed."

"What don't you like about her now?"

"She's *too* independent and strong-willed. She doesn't need me. She's still as beautiful as ever, but other guys are attracted to her."

"So the qualities that you found attractive are now objectionable to you? Is that why you put her down?"

"It's not that I object to them. But she's got to be put in her place from time to time."

"And what is her place?"

"I want her to remember that she's my wife and that when she comes on strong it doesn't do a hell of a lot for me."

When I talked with Sharon, she confided that she also put him down. "What do you gain by doing that?" I asked.

"I don't want him to feel he's better than me, that's all."

"Why did you marry Harvey?"

"He was ambitious, outgoing, confident of himself, and knew what he wanted from life."

"Has he lost any of these qualities?"

"He's just too sure of himself and the life of the party. How do you think that makes me feel?"

"I don't know. How does it make you feel?"

"It makes me feel like I'm nobody. So I put him down just to let him know he can't get away with it."

Here is a situation in which the very qualities which attracted two people to each other are now criticized. Each partner is fighting and competing for first place, rather than working toward a complementary partnership where both win.

Another couple I know well has managed to avoid a competitive relationship by developing attitudes based on mutual support and acknowledgment. Al boasts of his wife's accomplishments as a novice tennis player, gardener, and cook. When they are with friends and any of these topics are discussed, Al, who is a successful stockbroker, sits back and listens. On occasion he will ask a question or two, as would any interested party. But he also supports his wife with encouraging comments and by offering his help when she needs it.

Mona, in turn, is proud of her husband's abilities in the world of finance and stocks. She does not tread on his area of specialty. Rather, she allows him to enjoy the limelight when he is "onstage." He also has the floor when his hobby of photography comes up in discussion. Mona even volunteers to show off some of his accomplishments when they have company. It is quite evident to their friends that Mona and Al consider themselves fortunate to have each other as partners.

By the way, when it comes to domestic decisions in which both feel they have an equal voice, they negotiate. These kinds of situations do not arise often because both have learned to trust each other's judgment. So when a problem or controversial issue arises, the decision is made by the person who feels most strongly one way or the other.

Giving Is Not Giving Up

One of the most common misconceptions about marriage is that each partner must make personal sacrifices for the other. I have heard this notion expressed with such statements as: "When you marry, you have to give up your freedom," or "I'm not ready to sacrifice my life for somebody else."

The term "sacrifice," when it is used in the context of personal relationships, turns me off. When a person claims he is sacrificing his life for another individual, he is implying that he is giving up some things without getting anything in return. The person who is making what he considers to be a sacrifice implies that he is on the short end of the stick, and that his actions represent a loss.

If that is what an individual means when he says, "You need to make sacrifices in marriage," he is deluding himself. Such persons are confusing *giving up* with *giving. When you give to a partner you receive some benefits from the act.* It may be a personal satisfaction or some other good feeling which the act provides. But, *when you give up you get absolutely nothing of value in return.* A self-sacrificial attitude is destructive to a marital relationship. The person doing the sacrificing usually feels cheated and resentful.

The first time I presented this idea to a group, one woman asked me, "What about someone like me who worked three years to put her husband through school? Wasn't that a sacrifice?"

"Are you saying that you got no pleasure from helping your husband?"

"Oh, sure I did," she replied. "It made me feel good to know that I was contributing to our future."

"Did you feel resentful about doing it?"

"No, not really. I rather enjoyed it."

"Then it wasn't a sacrifice. You worked because it was an investment toward what you believed to be some worthwhile future dividends. Furthermore, you liked what you were doing. So what was the sacrifice?"

Apparently there wasn't any, at least not in that situation.

Not all circumstances are as clear-cut as this one. Many men and women insist on being self-sacrificial, and then become resentful toward their spouse because they feel they are missing out on their good times. I have known men, for example, who have told me, "I used to play ball on Sunday mornings with the boys, but I don't do that any more because I feel I should be with the family." Or, "I used to enjoy camping on a weekend, but my wife doesn't, so I haven't done it since we married." From wives I have heard such complaints as, "I want to go to work, because I enjoy it, but my husband won't let me." Or "I always wanted to take a course in _____, but my husband thinks that's silly."

These seemingly self-sacrificial gestures, which are really attempts to maintain domestic tranquility, build walls between couples. When you submit to unreasonable demands, which make you feel that you are giving up those things that are important to you, you are shortchanging yourself and your partner. *In order to invest fully in your partner, you must also invest in yourself.*

Thanks to my wife, I learned this lesson early in our marriage. I was to go in for surgery on a Wednesday morning. About one hour before the operation Joan came to visit me. To my surprise she was wearing a brand-new dress. "When did you get it?" I asked.

"Yesterday afternoon."

"I don't understand," I retorted. "Here I am going in for surgery and you bought yourself a dress? This doesn't call for a celebration, you know."

To this she replied, "I know that when you get out you'll need a lot of attention and care. And I'm prepared to give all of myself to you. I felt I needed something to bolster my own spirits, so I bought the dress. Do you understand?"

Her explanation not only made sense, but it taught me one of the most important principles I have learned over the years: *You can't give to others until you first give to yourself.* When you continue to sacrifice your personal desires in the interest of pleasing your spouse, you eventually run dry. I don't believe that's the kind of person your partner would want.

19

Communication in Marriage

Would you accept a responsible job with a company without knowing what was expected from you? If you did, you would be placing yourself in a position of constantly playing guessing games. Out of sheer desperation you would do all kinds of things hoping to please your boss, with no assurance that you were on the right track. Because your guesses might be wrong, you would be subject to constant criticism. Without knowing what was expected from you, your chances of failing on the job would be great.

Because progressive companies know this, they provide their responsible employees with guidelines that define the nature of the job and describe the expectations or the bases on which the company will evaluate an employee's performance. Such guidelines reduce the "I didn't know I was responsible for this" type of disagreements and allow the employee to determine for himself whether he is fulfilling the obligations that will yield the rewards he is seeking from his job.

Sensible as this idea sounds, couples may go on for years not knowing what each expects or wants from the other. It's not that they don't have expectations of each other. Of course they do. But these desires are rarely, if ever, voiced. Because of this lack of communication, they will argue and express disappointment when their expectations are not fulfilled.

Many feel that one partner should instinctively know what

194

the other partner wants, needs, or expects without any clues. "If he doesn't know, I won't tell him," a frequent reaction, becomes a trap in which both parties wind up losing.

Partners who do not have their desires fulfilled because they fail to make their expectations known eventually develop the attitude that their spouse can't be counted on for anything. This negative prophecy often becomes self-fulfilling, as each works diligently in what turns out to be mutual sabotage.

Take the case of Keith and Marilyn, who discussed their problem in my office:

Marilyn: Ever since we've been married we hardly ever go out together.
Keith: I thought she liked to stay home because she is so busy with meetings and other things during the week. Most of the time she's tired. She never suggested going out.
Marilyn: I thought *you* were the one who didn't want to go out, so I didn't bug you about it.
Keith: Okay, how about you and I going to a movie tonight?
Marilyn: I have a meeting tonight.
Keith: That's why I don't ask her.
Marilyn: It figures that he would ask me when I can't make it.

Neither one made a move toward suggesting another day. They have both become so accustomed to being disappointed by each other that they have given up the effort to find out what it takes to please their partner. How can two people fulfill each other's desires when they don't communicate them? As it turned out, both Keith and Marilyn wanted to go out, so I suggested they make a date they could agree upon.

Couples who have a wholesome marital relationship communicate honestly with each other, and have learned to sense each other's desires. They have also learned how to express disappointments appropriately when these occur. How does a couple *develop an effective climate for expressing mutual expecta-*

tions and wants? They must make a *cooperative* effort; otherwise it won't work.

1. The first step is for both of you to *write down,* on separate sheets of paper and without any discussion, *all the things you expect from your spouse.* You may find it helpful to think in terms of categories such as: domestic responsibilities, handling of children, personal-sexual relationship, general attitudes, and emotional honesty. Under each of these, or any other general categories you may choose, explain your desires—*be specific* in your statements. For example, "I expect to have dinner on time" is preferable to "I expect you to be a good housewife"—that's too general. Or "I expect to have time alone with you after dinner, and without interruption," is preferred over "We need more time together." Be sure to list all your major expectations.

2. Next to each statement *indicate whether the particular expectation is fulfilled (F), partially fulfilled (P), or unfulfilled (U).* The reason I'm suggesting you list the fulfilled, as well as the partially and the totally unfulfilled, expectations is that we don't want the discussion that will follow to be a pure gripe session. After all, your spouse does some things right, so give your partner recognition for these actions.

3. When both of you have completed your lists you are ready to *begin your discussions.* Since this is the most crucial and delicate part of your program to increase your understanding of each other, it has to be done carefully. Here are some guidelines which will aid you in the process:

a. Conduct your discussions when both of you have time and are fairly free of pressures. The whole list need not be discussed in one sitting.

b. These are problem-solving discussions. Do not make them into mutual accusation sessions. You are interested in improving conditions, rather than finding fault.

c. When an expectation is stated as being partially fulfilled or unfulfilled, do not take a defensive posture. Your purpose is to exchange information. "Why," "how," and "when" questions will help you to achieve that objective.

d. When an unfulfilled expectation is stated don't retaliate with "But *you* don't" statements. You'll get your turn to express your desires.

With these guidelines in mind, whoever decides to start does so by first reading and elaborating on all the *fulfilled* expecta- ' tions. Next, choose one of your more important unfulfilled expectations and read it. Then determine whether this expectation is legitimate or not. This is vital. If, in your partner's opinion, it is not legitimate, find out why. You might need to reevaluate this expectation, and even modify it.

Assuming you are now talking about a desire which your spouse agrees is reasonable, offer one or two reasons for wanting this expectation fulfilled. You might also let your partner know how you feel when this desire is not met. Let us say, for example, that a husband says, "I would like, if you're on the phone when I come home from work, for you to end the conversation quickly and acknowledge my presence." He elaborates on his request by adding: "I look forward to coming home, and I would like to believe that you are eager to see me. But when you remain on the phone for a good half hour after I arrive, I feel that you don't care whether or not I'm here."

Having stated and explained your desire, you are now ready to arrive at some mutually agreeable solution or promise. In the above example the wife agreed to make every effort not to be on the phone when her husband came home. She also promised that if, when he arrived, she happened to be discussing an important matter on the telephone, she would inform him of this fact. He accepted her promise, and that problem was solved.

The final step in discussing each expectation is not always as clear-cut as the telephone problem might suggest. In many instances one partner is able to fulfill the other's request only under certain conditions, as is illustrated in the following dialogue:

Wife: When something is bothering you, and I ask you about it, I would like you to tell me. But, you don't.

Instead, you keep it in and walk around looking like the world is coming to an end.

Husband: In the past, when I've told you what was on my mind, you've lectured me. I don't like to be lectured to. That's why I don't tell you when I'm bugged. I figure I've got enough problems without you talking down to me.

Wife: I don't mean to lecture you. All I want to do is help.

Husband: I don't want that kind of help. If I wanted your advice I'd ask for it. Sometimes I just want someone to listen without saying anything back to me.

Wife: If I promise to do that, and to give you my reaction only when you ask me, will you tell me what's bothering you?

Husband: Okay. I'll level with you, but only on that condition. And if you start in on me—

Wife: If I start in on you, just remind me what I promised.

Husband: That's a deal.

After the person who has begun is satisfied with the agreement or solution, the other partner takes his or her first turn. Just as your spouse had done earlier, read all your fulfilled expectations and then proceed with your major unfulfilled desire. Remember to follow the guidelines and to take turns. Again, this process may take a considerable amount of time. But when you finish, both of you will have a better understanding of what it takes to satisfy your partner.

While I have recommended that you be complete in developing your list of desires, I know from experience that some expectations are hidden and cannot be voiced. These would be more appropriately classified as hopes rather than expectations. A wife, for example, might *hope* that if she's extremely tired her husband will offer to do the dishes. And, a husband might *hope* that his wife is in a romantic mood on a particular Sunday afternoon. Neither necessarily *expects* these spontaneous gestures, but they would be viewed as bonuses. And, in most instances, bonuses are pleasant surprises which say, in effect, "I care enough for you to do *more* than you expect." Think about these bonuses in relation to your spouse. They can make the difference between a so-so relationship and a good one.

Over the years I have collected some hidden expectations which were expressed to me by both men and women. I offer them to you as food for thought.

What Women Expect from Their Husbands

—I don't want him to make me feel that he is the only one who works. My work at home is as important as what he does.

—I expect him to support me emotionally when I'm ill, and to take over in a calm and silent manner. Just the calming influence of someone who cares when I am sick helps a lot.

—I expect him to be warmly affectionate and sincerely interested in me—not only as a marriage partner, but as an enjoyable human being.

—I expect him to show me the common courtesy he shows other people.

—I expect him to stand up for what he believes to be right, but also to be flexible enough to welcome new and different ideas or thoughts.

—I expect him to really be with me when we are together and to concentrate on *us* at those times.

—I would like unsought thanks for the many extras I provide —extra baking, a button sewn on promptly, etc. A rose for no reason at all or a book which I said I would really like to have would be a welcome surprise.

—I expect him to sense my mood and adjust to it, rather than push me when I am discouraged or really tired.

—I expect his criticism to be constructive and to be done in a kind way.

—I expect him to protect me (verbally) from anyone who might try to hurt or abuse me.

What Men Expect from Their Wives

—I expect her to be well poised and at ease in a variety of situations.

—I expect her to have a basic understanding of the problems I face every day, and to realize how they affect us.

—I expect her to face problems in a realistic manner without copping out.

—I expect her to know and decide what she wants out of life, both as an individual and as a wife. I don't want her to depend on me for everything.

—I would like her to show some initiative sexually; I don't want to be the one that always does the asking.

—I expect her to show some interest in those things that are important to me—my job, hobbies, etc.

—I expect her to effectively manage those things which are within her area of responsibility, and to maintain control over them.

—I expect her to be honest with me about her feelings and not use our sexual relationship as a weapon.

—I expect her to back me up in my decisions concerning the children, and to discuss areas we don't agree upon.

—I expect her to let me know, in her own way, that I have a friend at home and not just a dependent whom I must support.

Isn't it interesting that so many of the wife's expectations could just as well be the husband's and vice versa?

An effective, "communicating" marriage has to be an ongoing process. This requires you to update and regularly discuss your desires. As people and circumstances change, so do their expectations. Furthermore, it is important that neither of you allows the other to violate your agreements. If a reasonable and agreed-upon expectation is not met, call your partner's attention to it. "What happened to our agreements?" might serve as a gentle reminder. By no means assume a quiet, "I knew it wouldn't work" attitude. People do forget, and need to be reminded. You've got to *maintain open lines of communication where feelings, ideas, and problems are discussed* in a way that is beneficial to both partners.

While these informal talks and meetings will undoubtedly help both you and your partner keep in touch with each other on a daily basis, let me recommend one specific activity which has long-term value: *inventory taking.*

Companies take inventory in order to determine what stock (personnel and merchandise) they have available and what they need to meet present and future market demands. Similarly, a marriage can flounder and go stale unless the principals take regular stock of their partnership. They need to inventory *where they are now, where they are going, where they want to go, and how they will arrive at their destination.*

When you take inventory, I suggest you be specific. Planning ahead, and looking at today in terms of the future, can be both interesting and fun. You may find some exciting ways of filling those voids that exist in your marriage. In effect, such an exercise, when done seriously, can provide you with some specific directions for building a mutually profitable venture.

Part 6

LOOKING AHEAD

20

A Prospectus for the Future

Few things in life are more inspiring than watching a true professional do what he does best. A professional manager who runs his department smoothly, a major-league baseball player who fields tough grounders in a seemingly effortless manner, a competitive swimmer who moves gracefully through the water —all are beautiful sights to behold. What makes these people professional is that *they use the skills and tools of their profession without being obvious about it.*

What the viewer doesn't see is all the practice, discipline, and tireless effort it takes to produce the results he pays to see. To us who enjoy their feats their accomplishments look easy; and that's the beauty of it. These individuals go about the business of doing their thing and producing profits for those who employ their services.

In the business of living people rarely, if ever, function as smoothly as a manager of a well-run organization, nor do they achieve the efficiency of a highly disciplined athlete in training. To expect such perfection is unrealistic. Both the manager and athlete have, in their respective functions, clearly defined products and services to offer. Their markets are defined, and both have the opportunity to obtain formal training in their specialties and to learn from experts who have preceded them.

Most of us, on the other hand, are not trained in the business of living. Conducting this business successfully is an art; there are no "right" and "wrong" methods. The dimensions and variables we have to contend with far exceed those of any skill imaginable, and there are no definitive answers to the human problems we face daily. We can't feed data into a "human problem-solver computer" in the hope of arriving at a clear course of action. For these very reasons the business of living is exciting and challenging, as well as uncertain and troublesome.

At best, we can work every day with the diligence of a manager, athlete, or performer, to learn as much as we can about the nature of our business. We can learn more effective ways of riding out the hard times we encounter. We can increase our sensitivity toward our continually changing "product," as well as the market conditions, and adapt to them.

You will be in the business of living until your sixties, seventies, or even eighties. *Living means dreaming about tomorrow, but also enjoying and getting the most out of today.* Simply dreaming without making a conscious effort to realize your dreams is fruitless; so is plodding along each day without dreams to strive for.

I've got two final questions I would like you to ask yourself: *"If I were a publicly owned company, would I buy stock in myself?"* If not, *"What can I do to increase my value to myself and others?"* In attempting to answer these questions you will hopefully remind yourself to regularly evaluate who you are, what you want, and where you are going.

You may need to reread sections of this book to help you. But you *can* make the future brighter than the past. Tomorrow is a new day; don't waste it. If you look for the "ponies," I assure you you'll find them. If you view the business of living as a full-time career whose success depends on you, perhaps you will take it more seriously.

How do I end a book whose subject has no ending? Normally you know a book has ended when you have read the last word of the last chapter. I prefer to believe, because I am a confirmed optimist, that the last page of *this* book is really the beginning. I would like to think that the real ending rests within you and the personal profits you will generate from the ideas I have shared with you. I also choose to believe that by enriching your own business you will elevate the quality of living of the people you come in contact with.

Do you share these beliefs with me? If so, let us begin.